California
Everyday Mathematics®

The University of Chicago School Mathematics Project

Student Math Journal
Volume 2

Grade 4

McGraw Hill **Wright Group**

The University of Chicago School Mathematics Project (UCSMP)

Max Bell, Director, UCSMP Elementary Materials Component; Director, *Everyday Mathematics* First Edition
James McBride, Director, *Everyday Mathematics* Second Edition
Andy Isaacs, Director, *Everyday Mathematics* Third Edition
Amy Dillard, Associate Director, *Everyday Mathematics* Third Edition

Authors

Max Bell	Andy Isaacs	Robert Balfanz*	Robert Hartfield
John Bretzlauf	James McBride	William Carroll*	Peter Saecker
Amy Dillard	Kathleen Pitvorec	Sheila Sconiers*	

First Edition only

Technical Art
Diana Barrie

Teachers in Residence
Carla L. LaRochelle, Rebecca W. Maxcy

Editorial Assistant
Laurie K. Thrasher

Photo Credits
© Gregory Adams/Getty Images, cover, *top right;* Getty Images, cover, *center;* ©Tony Hamblin; Frank Lane Picture Agency/CORBIS, cover, *bottom left;* ©Nick Rowe/Getty Images, p. v.

Contributors
Martha Ayala, Virginia J. Bates, Randee Blair, Donna R. Clay, Vanessa Day, Jean Faszholz, James Flanders, Patti Haney, Margaret Phillips Holm, Nancy Kay Hubert, Sybil Johnson, Judith Kiehm, Deborah Arron Leslie, Laura Ann Luczak, Mary O'Boyle, William D. Pattison, Beverly Pilchman, Denise Porter, Judith Ann Robb, Mary Seymour, Laura A. Sunseri-Driscoll

This material is based upon work supported by the National Science Foundation under Grant No. ESI-9252984. Any opinions, findings, conclusions, or recommendations expressed in this material are those of the authors and do not necessarily reflect the views of the National Science Foundation.

California *Everyday Mathematics* Reviewers

Dr. Dale Oliver, Humboldt State University
Dr. Bill Jacobs, University of California, Santa Barbara

Dr. Elizabeth Burroughs, Humboldt State University
Dr. Alfred Manaster, University of California, San Diego

www.WrightGroup.com

Wright Group

Printed in the United States of America.

Send all inquiries to:
Wright Group/McGraw-Hill
P.O. Box 812960
Chicago, IL 60681

ISBN 978-0-07-609817-0
MHID 0-07-609817-6

6 7 8 9 QDB 13 12 11

The McGraw·Hill Companies

Contents

UNIT 7 Fractions and Their Uses; Chance and Probability

UNIT 8 Perimeter and Area

UNIT 11   3-D Shapes, Weight, Volume, and Capacity

UNIT 12 Rates

Activity Sheets

LESSON 7·1 Fraction Review

Divide each shape into equal parts. Color a
fraction of the parts. Write the name of the
"whole" in the **"whole"** box.

1. | **Whole** |
| *hexagon* |

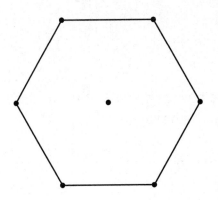

Divide the hexagon into 2 equal parts.
Color $\frac{1}{2}$ of the hexagon.

2. | **Whole** |
| |

Divide the rhombus into 2 equal parts.
Color $\frac{0}{2}$ of the rhombus.

3. | **Whole** |
| |

Divide the trapezoid into 3 equal parts.
Color $\frac{2}{3}$ of the trapezoid.

4. | **Whole** |
| |

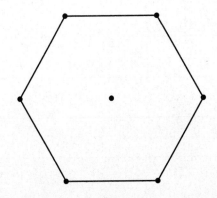

Divide the hexagon into 3 equal parts.
Color $\frac{1}{3}$ of the hexagon.

LESSON 7·1 **Fraction Review** *continued*

5. **Whole**

hexagon

Divide the hexagon into 6 equal parts.
Color $\frac{5}{6}$ of the hexagon.

6. **Whole**

hexagon

Divide each hexagon into thirds.
Color $1\frac{2}{3}$ hexagons.

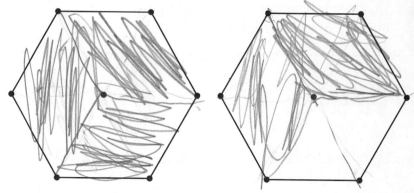

7. **Whole**

rhombus

Divide each rhombus into 2 equal parts.
Color $2\frac{1}{2}$ rhombuses.

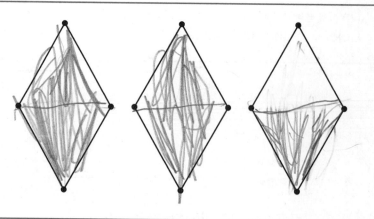

8. Grace was asked to color $\frac{2}{3}$ of a hexagon.
This is what she did. What is wrong?

Grace cut the thirds wrong.

Number Sense 1.5; Number Sense 1.7; Mathematical Reasoning 2.3

LESSON 7·1 **Fraction Review** *continued*

Fill in the missing fractions and mixed numbers on the number lines.

9.

0     $\frac{1}{4}$ $\frac{2}{4}$ $\frac{3}{4}$ 1

10.

0     $\frac{1}{3}$ $\frac{2}{3}$ 1

11.

0   $\frac{1}{6}$ $\frac{2}{6}$ $\frac{3}{6}$ $\frac{4}{6}$ $\frac{5}{6}$ 1

12.

0   $\frac{1}{8}$ $\frac{2}{8}$ $\frac{3}{8}$ $\frac{4}{8}$ $\frac{5}{8}$ $\frac{6}{8}$ $\frac{7}{8}$ 1

13.

0   $\frac{1}{2}$ 1 $1\frac{1}{2}$ 2 $2\frac{1}{2}$ 3

14.

0   $\frac{1}{5}$ $\frac{2}{5}$ $\frac{3}{5}$ $\frac{4}{5}$ 1 $1\frac{1}{5}$ $1\frac{2}{5}$ $1\frac{3}{5}$ $1\frac{4}{5}$ 2

Try This

15. Enter the fractions above on your calculator. Record the keystrokes you used to enter $\frac{2}{4}$ and $1\frac{1}{5}$.

$2 \div 4 = 0.5$ $1 \div 1 \div 5 = 0.2$ $1 \times 5 = 5 + 1 = \frac{6}{5} = 1.2$

_____

_____

_____

Number Sense 1.5; Number Sense 1.9   **187**

LESSON 7·1

Math Boxes

---

1. What fraction of the clock face is shaded?

_____

SRB
56

2. ∠POL is an _____ (acute or obtuse) angle.

The measure of ∠POL is

°

_____.

SRB
93 142
143

---

3. Multiply. Use a paper-and-pencil algorithm.

_____ = 94 * 34

SRB
18 19

4. The five largest birds that are able to fly have the following weights: 16.3, 16.8, 20.9, 15.8, and 15.8 kilograms.

a. What is the median weight? _____ kg

b. What is the mode? _____ kg

c. What is the range? _____ kg

d. What is the mean? _____ kg

SRB
73 75

---

5. a. What city in Region 1 is located near 30°N latitude and 31°E longitude?

_____

b. In which country is the city located?

_____

c. On which continent is the city located?

_____

SRB
282 283

6. a. Measure and record the length of each side of the rectangle.

_____ in.

_____ in.   _____ in.

_____ in.

b. What is the total distance around the rectangle called? Circle one.

perimeter   area

SRB
131

---

1) NS 1.7   2) MG 3.5   3) NS 3.2
4) SDAP 1.2   5) MR 2.0   6) MG 1.0

LESSON 7·2   "Fraction-of" Problems

SRB
59

1. **Whole**

16 nickels

a. Circle $\frac{3}{4}$ of the nickels.

b. How much money is that?

$_____._____

2. **Whole**

a. Fill in the "whole" box.

b. Circle $\frac{5}{6}$ of the dimes.
How much money is that?

$_____._____

3. **Whole**

a. Fill in the "whole" box.

b. Circle $\frac{3}{5}$ of the quarters.
How much money is that?

$_____._____

Date _____ Time _____

"Fraction-of" Problems *continued*

Solve.

4. a. $\frac{1}{3}$ of 12 = _____4_____   b. $\frac{2}{3}$ of 12 = _____8_____   c. $\frac{5}{3}$ of 12 = _____

5. a. $\frac{1}{5}$ of 15 = _____3_____   b. $\frac{3}{5}$ of 15 = _____6_____   c. $\frac{7}{5}$ of 15 = _____

6. a. $\frac{1}{4}$ of 36 = _____9_____   b. $\frac{3}{4}$ of 36 = _____18_____   c. $\frac{6}{4}$ of 36 = _____216_____

7. a. $\frac{1}{8}$ of 32 = _____4_____   b. $\frac{5}{8}$ of 32 = _____8_____   c. $\frac{9}{8}$ of 32 = _____

8. a. $\frac{1}{6}$ of 24 = _____4_____   b. $\frac{4}{6}$ of 24 = _____   c. $\frac{13}{6}$ of 24 = _____

9. $\frac{2}{4}$ of 14 = _____3_____

10. $\frac{2}{4}$ of 22 = _____5_____

11. What is $\frac{1}{2}$ of 25? _____ Explain.

_____

_____

12. Michael had 20 baseball cards. He gave $\frac{1}{5}$ of them to his friend Alana, and $\frac{2}{5}$ to his brother Dean.

   a. How many baseball cards did he give to Alana? _____ cards

   b. How many did he give to Dean? _____ cards

   c. How many did he keep for himself? _____ cards

Try This

13. Maurice spent $\frac{1}{2}$ of his money on lunch. He has $2.50 left.

   How much money did he start with? _____

14. Erika spent $\frac{3}{4}$ of her money on lunch. She has $2.00 left.

   How much money did she start with? _____

Number Sense 1.7; Number Sense 1.5

Math Boxes

1. What fraction of the clock face is shaded? Fill in the circle next to the best answer.

Ⓐ $\frac{1}{3}$

Ⓑ $\frac{6}{12}$

Ⓒ $\frac{1}{4}$

Ⓓ $\frac{2}{1}$

2. Draw angle *ABC* that measures 65°.

∠*ABC* is an _____ (acute or obtuse) angle.

3. Mary has 27 pictures. She gives $\frac{1}{3}$ of them to her sister Barb and $\frac{2}{3}$ to her cousin Sara.

a. How many pictures does Barb get?

_____ pictures

b. How many pictures does Sara get?

_____ pictures

c. How many pictures does Mary keep?

_____ pictures

4. Divide. Use a paper-and-pencil algorithm.

962 / 12 = _____

5. There are 29 students in Ms. Wright's class. Each collected 50 bottle caps. How many bottle caps did the students collect in all?

_____ bottle caps

6. Find the area of the figure.

☐ = 1 square centimeter

Area = _____ square cm

LESSON 7·3 Playing Card Probabilities

A deck of regular playing cards is placed in a bag. You shake the bag and, without looking, pick one card.

1. How many possible outcomes are there?
   (*Hint:* How many cards are in the bag?) _____ possible outcomes

2. Are the outcomes equally likely?
   (*Hint:* Does each card have an equal chance of being chosen?) _____

3. Find the probability of each event. Probability of an event $= \dfrac{\text{number of favorable outcomes}}{\text{number of possible outcomes}}$

Event	Favorable Outcomes	Possible Outcomes	Probability
Pick a red card	26	52	$\dfrac{26}{52}$
Pick a club	13	52	$\dfrac{13}{52}$
Pick a non-face card	40	52	$\dfrac{40}{52}$
Pick a diamond face card	39	52	
Pick a card that is *not* a diamond face card	49	52	$\dfrac{49}{52}$
Pick the ace of clubs	1	52	$\dfrac{1}{52}$
Pick a red *or* a black card	52	52	$\dfrac{52}{52}$
Pick the 23 of hearts	0	52	$\dfrac{0}{52}$

4. Circle the word or phrase that best describes the probability of picking a 5 from a bag of 52 regular playing cards without looking.

   impossible   very unlikely   (even chance)   likely

   Explain why you chose your answer. _I chose my answer_ _because theres 4 cards of 5. there are dimonds heart, clubs and spad. theres a possible chance_

Statistics, Data Analysis, and Probability 2.1; Statistics, Data Analysis, and Probability 2.2

LESSON 7·3 — Math Boxes

1. What fraction of the clock face is shaded?

_____

SRB
56

2. ∠*MRS* is an _____ (acute or obtuse) angle.

The measure of ∠*MRS* is
_____ °.

SRB
93 142
143

3. Multiply. Use a paper-and-pencil algorithm.

_____ = 19 ∗ 473

SRB
18 19

4. Cleo's friends ran the 50-yard dash in the following times:

7.9, 12.1, 8.5, 11.7, 8.3, 11.7,
and 9.8 seconds.

What is the mean time? Fill in the circle next to the best answer.

Ⓐ 11.7 seconds

Ⓑ 9.8 seconds

Ⓒ 10 seconds

Ⓓ 12.1 seconds

SRB
73–75

5. **a.** What city in Region 2 is located near 60°N latitude and 10°E longitude?

_____

b. In which country is the city located?

_____

c. On which continent is the city located?

_____

SRB
284 285

6. Measure the length and width of your journal to the nearest half-inch. Find its perimeter.

a. Length = _____ inches

b. Width = _____ inches

c. Perimeter = _____ inches

SRB
131

LESSON 7·4

Pattern-Block Fractions

Use *Math Masters,* page 212. For Problems 1–6, Shape A is the whole.

1. Cover Shape A with trapezoid blocks. What fraction of the shape is covered by 1 trapezoid? $\frac{1}{2}$

2. Cover Shape A with rhombuses. What fraction of the shape is covered by

   1 rhombus? $\frac{1}{3}$

   2 rhombuses? $\frac{2}{3}$

3. Cover Shape A with triangles. What fraction of the shape is covered by

   1 triangle? $\frac{1}{6}$

   3 triangles? $\frac{3}{6}$

   5 triangles? $\frac{5}{6}$

4. Cover Shape A with 1 trapezoid and 3 triangles. With a straightedge, draw how your shapes look on the hexagon at the right. Label each part with a fraction.

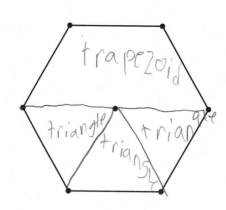

5. Cover Shape A with 2 rhombuses and 2 triangles. Draw the result on the hexagon below. Label each part with a fraction.

6. Cover Shape A with 1 trapezoid, 1 rhombus, and 1 triangle. Draw the result on the hexagon below. Label each part with a fraction.

Number Sense 1.5; Number Sense 1.7; Measurement and Geometry 3.0

LESSON 7·4 **Pattern-Block Fractions** *continued*

Use *Math Masters,* page 212. For Problems 7–12, Shape B is the whole.

> **Whole**
> Shape B:
> double hexagon

7. Cover Shape B with trapezoids.
    What fraction of the shape is covered by

    1 trapezoid? __$\frac{1}{4}$__   2 trapezoids? __$\frac{2}{4}$__   3 trapezoids? __$\frac{2}{4}$__

8. Cover Shape B with rhombuses. What fraction of the shape is covered by

    1 rhombus? __$\frac{1}{6}$__   3 rhombuses? __$\frac{3}{6}$__   5 rhombuses? __$\frac{5}{6}$__

9. Cover Shape B with triangles. What fraction of the shape is covered by

    1 triangle? __$\frac{1}{12}$__   2 triangles? __$\frac{2}{12}$__   3 triangles? __$\frac{3}{12}$__

10. Cover Shape B with hexagons. What fraction of the shape is covered by

    1 hexagon? __$\frac{1}{2}$__   2 hexagons? __$\frac{2}{2}$__

11. Cover Shape B completely
    with 1 hexagon, 1 rhombus,
    1 triangle, and 1 trapezoid.
    Draw the result on the figure
    at the right. Label each part
    with a fraction.

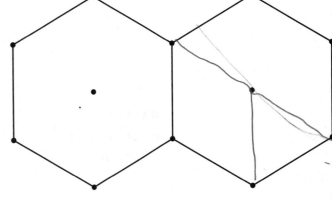

12. Cover Shape B completely
    with 1 trapezoid, 2 rhombuses,
    and 5 triangles. Draw the
    result on the figure at the right.
    Label each part with a fraction.

Number Sense 1.5; Number Sense 1.7; Measurement Frand Geometry 3.0

Date _____   Time _____

Pattern-Block Fractions *continued*

Use *Math Masters,* page 212. For Problems 13–16, Shape C is the whole.

Whole
Shape C:
big hexagon

Try This

13. Cover Shape C with trapezoids.
    What fraction of the shape is covered by

    1 trapezoid? $\frac{1}{8}$ 2 trapezoids? $\frac{2}{8}$ 6 trapezoids? $\frac{6}{8}$

14. Cover Shape C with rhombuses. What fraction of the shape is covered by

    1 rhombus? $\frac{1}{12}$ 3 rhombuses? $\frac{3}{12}$ 6 rhombuses? $\frac{6}{12}$

15. Cover Shape C with triangles. What fraction of the shape is covered by

    1 triangle? $\frac{1}{24}$ 3 triangles? $\frac{3}{24}$ 12 triangles? $\frac{12}{24}$

16. Cover Shape C completely, using one or more trapezoids, rhombuses, triangles, and
    hexagons. Draw the result on the big hexagon below. Label each part with a fraction.

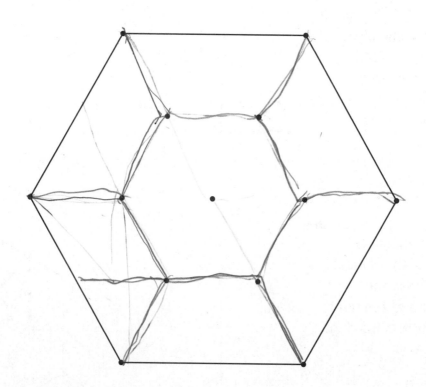

Number Sense 1.5; Number Sense 1.7; Measurement and Geometry 3.0; Mathematical Reasoning 2.2

LESSON 7·4   **Math Boxes**

---

1. What fraction of the clock face is shaded?

_____

SRB 56

2. Draw angle *LMN* that measures 120°.

∠*LMN* is an _____
(acute or obtuse) angle.

SRB 93 142 143

---

3. **a.** In December, $\frac{3}{4}$ of a foot of snow fell on Wintersville. How many inches of snow fell?

_____ inches

b. Tina's daughter will be $\frac{5}{6}$ of a year old next week. How many months old will she be?

_____ months

SRB 59

4. Divide. Use a paper-and-pencil algorithm.

809 / 13 = _____

SRB 22 23 179

---

5. Each student eats an average of 17 servings of junk food per week. About how many servings of junk food would a class of 32 students eat in a week?

_____ servings

6. Find the area of the figure.

☐ = 1 square centimeter

Area = _____ square cm

SRB 133

LESSON 7·5   Pattern-Block Fraction Sums & Differences

1. Use pattern blocks to find fractions that add up to 1 whole. Draw lines to show the blocks you used. Write a number model to show that the sum of your fractions is 1.

Whole

hexagon

55

$\frac{1}{6} + \frac{1}{6} + \frac{1}{3} + \frac{1}{3} = 1$ _____   _____

_____   _____   _____

2. Use pattern blocks to find fractions that add up to $\frac{2}{3}$. Draw lines to show the blocks you used. Write a number model to show that the sum of your fractions is $\frac{2}{3}$.

_____   _____   _____

Solve. You may use pattern blocks or any other method.

3. $\frac{2}{3} - \frac{1}{6} =$ _____

4. $\frac{5}{6} - \frac{1}{2} =$ _____

5. $1\frac{1}{6} - \frac{1}{3} =$ _____

6. $1\frac{1}{2} - \frac{5}{6} =$ _____

Number Sense 1.5; Number Sense 1.7; Measurement and Geometry 3.0

LESSON 7·5 **Math Boxes**

---

1. Circle $\frac{1}{5}$ of all the triangles. Mark Xs on $\frac{2}{3}$ of all the triangles.

59

2. Insert parentheses to make these number sentences true.

a. $8.2 - 5.2 + 2.5 = 0.5$

b. $13.6 - 5 + 8 = 0.6$

c. $9.1 = 28.4 - 1.1 \div 3$

d. $9 * 2.5 + 3.5 = 54$

150

---

3. Plot and label each point on the coordinate grid.

A (5,0)

B (3,5)

C (1,4)

D (1,1)

E (2,4)

144

4. Draw and label a 45° angle.

This angle is an _____ (acute or obtuse) angle.

93 143

---

5. A bag contains

6 red blocks,
4 blue blocks,
7 green blocks, and
3 orange blocks.

You put your hand in the bag and, without looking, pull out a block. About what fraction of the time would you expect to get a blue block?

_____

45

6. If 1 centimeter on a map represents 10 kilometers, then

a. 6 cm represent _____ km.

b. 19.5 cm represent _____ km.

c. _____ cm represent 30 km.

d. _____ cm represent 55 km.

e. _____ cm represent 5 km.

145

Math Boxes

---

1. Which fraction is another name for $\frac{6}{8}$? Fill in the circle next to the best answer.

Ⓐ $\frac{1}{2}$

Ⓑ $\frac{3}{4}$

Ⓒ $\frac{4}{12}$

Ⓓ $\frac{2}{4}$

SRB
51

---

2. A bag contains

2 blue blocks,
3 red blocks,
5 green blocks, and
10 black blocks.

You put your hand in the bag and, without looking, pull out a block. About what fraction of the time would you expect to get a black block?

_____

SRB
45

---

3. Use pattern blocks to help you solve these problems.

a. $\frac{2}{6} + \frac{2}{6} =$ _____

b. $\frac{1}{2} + \frac{1}{3} =$ _____

c. $\frac{2}{3} - \frac{1}{3} =$ _____

d. $\frac{2}{3} - \frac{1}{6} =$ _____

SRB
55–57

---

4. $\angle TAP$ is an _____ (acute or obtuse) angle.

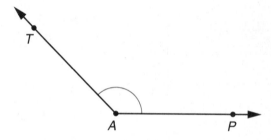

The measure of $\angle TAP$ is

_____ °.

SRB
93 142
143

---

5. Next month 486 students, teachers, and parents are going on a field trip to the zoo. Each bus holds 35 people. How many buses are needed for the trip?

_____ buses

---

6. Tell if each of these is closest to 1 inch, 1 foot, or 1 yard.

a. the length of your smile _____

b. the length
of your journal _____

c. the distance from
your waist to your feet _____

d. the width of your wrist _____

SRB
130

LESSON 7·7 Many Names for Fractions

Color the squares and write the missing numerators.

Whole
square

1. Color $\frac{1}{2}$ of each large square.

$\dfrac{1}{2}$ is colored.

$\dfrac{2}{4}$ is colored.

$\dfrac{4}{8}$ is colored.

2. Color $\frac{1}{4}$ of each large square.

$\dfrac{1}{4}$ is colored.

$\dfrac{2}{8}$ is colored.

$\dfrac{4}{16}$ is colored.

3. Color $\frac{3}{4}$ of each large square.

$\dfrac{3}{4}$ is colored.

$\dfrac{6 \div 2}{8 \div 2} \quad \dfrac{3}{4}$

$\dfrac{6}{8}$ is colored.

$\dfrac{6}{8} \times \dfrac{2}{2} =$

$\dfrac{12}{16}$ is colored.

LESSON 7·7 **Math Boxes**

---

1. Circle $\frac{3}{8}$ of all the squares. Mark Xs on $\frac{1}{6}$ of all the squares.

SRB 59

2. Insert parentheses to make these number sentences true.

a. $2 * 3 + 10 = 26$

b. $12 = 6 * 6 - 4$

c. $24 - 5 * 2 = 38$

d. $12 + 24 = 3 * 6 + 6$

SRB 150

---

3. Plot and label each point on the coordinate grid.

A $(0,2)$

B $(4,0)$

C $(1,5)$

D $(5,5)$

E $(5,3)$

SRB 144

4. Draw and label a 125° angle.

This angle is an _____
(acute or obtuse) angle.

SRB 92 93 143

---

5. A bag contains

5 green blocks,
6 red blocks,
1 blue block, and
3 yellow blocks.

You put your hand in the bag and, without looking, pull out a block. About what fraction of the time would you expect to get a blue block?

_____

SRB 45

6. If 1 inch on a map represents 40 miles, then how many inches represent 10 miles? Fill in the circle next to the best answer.

Ⓐ 2 in.

Ⓑ $\frac{1}{4}$ in.

Ⓒ $\frac{1}{2}$ in.

Ⓓ 4 in.

SRB 145

---

1) NS 1.7   2) AF 1.3   3) MG 2.0
4) MG 3.5   5) SDAP 2.2   6) AF 1.4

LESSON 7·8 Fractions and Decimals

Whole

large square

$\frac{1}{10}$, or 0.1

1.

$\frac{2}{10}$ of the square is shaded.

How many tenths? __2__

$\frac{2}{10}$ = 0.__2__

2.

$\frac{1}{2}$ is shaded.

How many tenths? __5__

$\frac{1}{2}$ = $\frac{\boxed{5}}{10}$ = 0.__5__

3.

$\frac{1}{5}$ is shaded.

How many tenths? __2__

$\frac{1}{5}$ = $\frac{\boxed{2}}{10}$ = 0.__2__

4.

$\frac{2}{5}$ is shaded.

How many tenths? __4__

$\frac{2}{5}$ = $\frac{\boxed{4}}{10}$ = 0.__4__

5. $\frac{3}{5}$ = $\frac{\boxed{6}}{10}$ = 0.__6__

6. $\frac{4}{5}$ = $\frac{\boxed{8}}{10}$ = 0.__8__

7.

$\frac{1}{4}$ is shaded.

$\frac{1}{4}$ = $\frac{\boxed{25}}{100}$ = 0.__25__

8.

$\frac{3}{4}$ is shaded.

$\frac{3}{4}$ = $\frac{\boxed{75}}{100}$ = 0.__75__

$\frac{1}{100}$, or 0.01

LESSON 7·8

Math Boxes

1. Complete the name-collection box.

$$\frac{4}{5}$$

SRB 51

2. A bag contains

8 blue blocks,
2 red blocks,
1 green block, and
4 orange blocks.

You put your hand in the bag and, without looking, pull out a block. About what fraction of the time would you expect to get a red block?

_____

SRB 45

3. Use pattern blocks to help you solve these problems.

a. $\frac{1}{3} + \frac{1}{3} =$ _____

b. $\frac{2}{6} + \frac{2}{3} =$ _____

c. $\frac{5}{6} - \frac{1}{6} =$ _____

d. $\frac{4}{6} - \frac{1}{2} =$ _____

SRB 55–57

4. ∠*ART* is an _____ (acute or obtuse) angle.

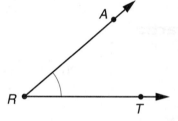

The measure of ∠*ART* is

_____°.

SRB 93 142 143

5. There are 252 pages in the book Ming is reading for his book report. He has two weeks to read the book. About how many pages should he read each day?

_____ pages

6. Tell if each of these is closest to 1 inch, 1 foot, or 1 yard.

a. the height of the door _____

b. the width of your journal _____

c. the length of your largest toe _____

d. the length of your shoe _____

SRB 130

1) NS 1.5   2) SDAP 2.2   3) MR 2.3
4) MG 3.5   5) MR 2.6   6) NS 1.4

LESSON
7·9

Comparing Fractions

Math Message: Eating Fractions

Quinn, Nancy, Diego, Paula, and Kiana were given 4 granola bars to share.
All 4 bars were the same size.

1. Quinn and Nancy shared a granola bar. Quinn ate $\frac{1}{4}$ of the bar, and Nancy ate $\frac{2}{4}$.

   Who ate more? _____

   How much of the bar was left? _____

2. Diego, Paula, and Kiana each ate part of the other granola bars. Diego ate $\frac{2}{3}$ of a bar, Paula ate $\frac{2}{5}$ of a bar, and Kiana ate $\frac{5}{6}$ of a bar.

   Who ate more, Diego or Paula? _____

   How do you know? _____

   _____

Comparing Fractions with $\frac{1}{2}$

Turn your Fraction Cards fraction-side up. Sort them into three piles:

   ◆ fractions less than $\frac{1}{2}$

   ◆ fractions equal to $\frac{1}{2}$

   ◆ fractions greater than $\frac{1}{2}$

You can turn the cards over to check your work. When you are finished,
write the fractions in each pile in the correct box below.

Less than $\frac{1}{2}$	**Equal to $\frac{1}{2}$**	**Greater than $\frac{1}{2}$**

LESSON 7·9 Ordering Fractions

Write the fractions in order from smallest to largest.

1. $\frac{4}{10}$, $\frac{7}{10}$, $\frac{8}{10}$, $\frac{2}{10}$, $\frac{1}{10}$

$\frac{1}{10}$ _____ $\frac{2}{10}$ _____ $\frac{4}{10}$ _____ $\frac{7}{10}$ _____ $\frac{8}{10}$ _____
smallest   **largest**

2. $\frac{1}{4}$, $\frac{1}{2}$, $\frac{1}{9}$, $\frac{1}{5}$, $\frac{1}{100}$

$\frac{1}{100}$ _____ $\frac{1}{9}$ _____ $\frac{1}{5}$ _____ $\frac{1}{4}$ _____ $\frac{1}{2}$ _____
smallest   **largest**

3. $\frac{2}{4}$, $\frac{2}{2}$, $\frac{2}{9}$, $\frac{2}{5}$, $\frac{2}{100}$

$\frac{2}{100}$ _____ $\frac{2}{9}$ _____ $\frac{2}{5}$ _____ $\frac{2}{4}$ _____ $\frac{2}{2}$ _____
smallest   **largest**

4. $\frac{4}{25}$, $\frac{1}{25}$, $\frac{7}{8}$, $\frac{6}{12}$, $\frac{7}{15}$

$\frac{1}{25}$ _____ $\frac{4}{25}$ _____ $\frac{7}{15}$ _____ $\frac{6}{12}$ _____ $\frac{7}{8}$ _____
smallest   **largest**

5. Choose 5 fractions or mixed numbers. Write them in order from smallest to largest.

$\frac{1}{100}$ _____ $\frac{2}{100}$ _____ $\frac{4}{15}$ _____ $\frac{1}{2}$ _____ $\frac{2}{2}$ _____
smallest   **largest**

6. Which fraction is larger: $\frac{2}{5}$ or $\frac{2}{7}$? $\frac{2}{5}$ Explain how you know.

$\frac{2}{5}$ is larger because 5 is lower
than 7 the lowest number is always
larger.

Number Sense 1.9

LESSON 7·9 **Math Boxes**

1. Sari spends $\frac{1}{3}$ of the day at school. Lunch, recess, music, gym, and art make up $\frac{1}{4}$ of her total time at school. How many hours are spent at these activities?

_____ hours

Show how you solved this problem.

$\frac{1}{4} \cdot of \frac{1}{3} = \frac{1}{12}$

_____

SRB 59

2. Multiply. Use a paper-and-pencil algorithm.

_____ 462 _____ = 92 ∗ 56

41
456
×92
462

SRB 18 19

3. Adena drew a line segment $\frac{3}{4}$ inch long. Then she erased $\frac{1}{2}$ inch. How long is the line segment now? Fill in the circle next to the best answer.

Ⓐ $\frac{4}{6}$ in.

Ⓑ $\frac{2}{2}$ in.

Ⓒ $\frac{1}{4}$ in.

Ⓓ $1\frac{1}{4}$ in.

SRB 55–57

4. Write an equivalent fraction, decimal, or whole number.

Decimal	Fraction
a. 0.40	_____
b. _____	$\frac{3}{10}$
c. _____	$\frac{100}{100}$
d. 0.6	_____

SRB 61 62

5. Complete the table and write the rule.

Rule: _____

in	out
6.19	11.92
12.03	
	8.99
	5.74
4.41	10.14

SRB 162–166

6. Complete.

a. 17 in. = _____ ft _____ in.

b. 43 in. = _____ ft _____ in.

c. 6 ft = _____ yd

d. 11 ft = _____ yd _____ ft

e. 73 yd = _____ ft

SRB 129

LESSON 7·10 What Is the ONE?

Math Message

1. If the triangle below is $\frac{1}{3}$, then what is the whole—the ONE? Draw it on the grid.

2. If $\frac{1}{4}$ of Mrs. Chin's class is 8 students, then
how many students does she have altogether? _____32_____ students

---

Use your Geometry Template to draw the answers for Problems 3–6.

3. If is $\frac{1}{2}$, then what is the ONE?

4. If is $\frac{1}{4}$, then what is the ONE?

5. If is $\frac{2}{3}$, then what is the ONE?

6. If is $\frac{2}{5}$, then what is the ONE?

Number Sense 1.5; Number Sense 1.7; Measurement and Geometry 3.0

LESSON 7·10 What is the ONE? *continued*

Solve. If you wish, draw pictures at the bottom of the page to help you solve the problems.

7. If ⭕⭕ / ⭕⭕⭕ is $\frac{1}{3}$, then what is the ONE? _____ counters

8. If ⭕⭕ / ⭕⭕ is $\frac{1}{4}$, then what is the ONE? _____ counters

9. If 10 counters are $\frac{2}{5}$, then what is the ONE? _____ counters

10. If 12 counters are $\frac{3}{4}$, then what is the ONE? _____ counters

11. If $\frac{1}{5}$ of the cookies that Mrs. Jackson baked is 12, then how many cookies did she bake in all? _____ cookies

12. In Mr. Mendez's class, $\frac{3}{4}$ of the students take music lessons. That is, 15 students take music lessons. How many students are in Mr. Mendez's class? _____ students

13. Explain how you solved Problem 12.

_____

_____

_____

_____

LESSON 7·10   **Math Boxes**

---

1. Name the shaded area as a fraction and a decimal.

   a. fraction:

   _____

   b. decimal:

   _____

   SRB
   27 61

2. Which number sentence is true? Fill in the circle next to the best answer.

   Ⓐ $\frac{5}{6} < \frac{1}{6}$

   Ⓑ $\frac{4}{10} > \frac{4}{5}$

   Ⓒ $\frac{1}{7} > \frac{1}{100}$

   Ⓓ $\frac{2}{12} = \frac{3}{6}$

   SRB
   53 54

---

3. Write 6 fractions equivalent to $\frac{14}{16}$.

   _____ _____

   _____ _____

   _____ _____

   SRB
   49–51

4. Divide. Use a paper-and-pencil algorithm.

   $\frac{723}{14} =$ _____

   SRB
   22 23
   179

---

5. Multiply. Use a paper-and-pencil algorithm.

   _____ = 68 * 124

   SRB
   18 19

6. Compare.

   a. 1 day is _____ times as long as 2 hours.

   b. 6 years is _____ times as long as 4 months.

   c. 3 gallons is _____ times as much as 8 cups.

   d. 8 cm is _____ times as long as 2 mm.

   e. 1 meter is _____ times as long as 2 cm.

   SRB
   315

---

1) NS 1.6   2) AF 1.0   3) NS 1.5
4) NS 3.2   5) NS 3.2   6) MR 1.2

LESSON 7·11 Making Spinners

1. Make a spinner. Color the circle in 6 different colors. Design the spinner so that the paper clip has the **same chance** of landing on each of the colors.

2. Make another spinner. Color the circle red, blue, and green so that the paper clip has

   ◆ a $\frac{1}{6}$ chance of landing on red

   and

   ◆ a $\frac{1}{3}$ chance of landing on blue.

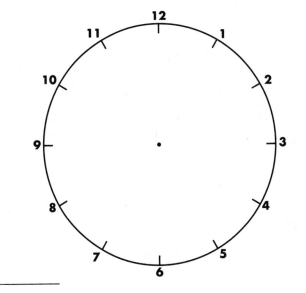

   a. What fraction of the circle did you color

      red? _____   blue? _____   green? _____

   b. Suppose you plan to spin the paper clip 24 times. About how many times would you expect it to land on

      red? _____   blue? _____   green? _____

   c. Suppose you plan to spin the paper clip 90 times. About how many times would you expect it to land on

      red? _____   blue? _____   green? _____

Math Boxes

1. According to a survey of 800 students at Martin Elementary, about $\frac{3}{4}$ of them chose pizza as their favorite food. Of those who chose pizza, $\frac{1}{2}$ liked pepperoni topping the best. How many students liked pepperoni topping the best?

_____ students

SRB
59

2. Multiply. Use a paper-and-pencil algorithm.

$71 * 38 =$ _____

SRB
18 19

3. a. Hannah drew a line segment $1\frac{5}{8}$ inches long. Then she erased $\frac{1}{2}$ inch. How long is the line segment now?

_____ inches

b. Joshua drew a line segment $\frac{7}{8}$ inch long. Then he added another $\frac{3}{4}$ inch. How long is the line segment now?

_____ inches

SRB
55–57

4. Write an equivalent fraction, decimal, or whole number.

Decimal	Fraction
a. 0.70	_____
b. _____	$\frac{25}{100}$
c. _____	$\frac{9}{9}$
d. 0.2	_____

SRB
61 62

5. Complete the table and write the rule.

Rule: _____

in	out
100.54	97.58
	52.95
72.03	
	67.44
59.21	56.25

SRB
162–166

6. Complete.

a. 5 ft = _____ yd _____ ft

b. 40 in. = _____ ft _____ in.

c. 80 in. = _____ yd _____ in.

d. 108 in. = _____ ft

e. $\frac{1}{3}$ yd = _____ in.

SRB
129

Expected Spinner Results

1. If this spinner is spun 24 times, how many times do you
   expect it to land on each color?

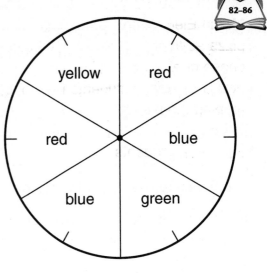

   a. Fill in the table.

Color	Expected Number in 24 Spins
red	
blue	
yellow	
green	
Total	**24**

   b. Explain how you determined the expected number of times the
      spinner would land on each color.

      _____

      _____

      _____

      _____

Try This

2. If a six-sided die is rolled 12 times, how many times would you expect to roll

   a. an odd number? _____

   b. a number less than 4? _____

   c. a 6? _____

   d. a square number? _____

   e. a triangular number? _____

   f. a prime number? _____

LESSON 7·12 — A Cube-Drop Experiment

Getting Ready

1. Follow the directions for coloring the grid on *Math Masters,* page 238. You may color the squares in any way. The colors can even form a pattern or a picture.

2. For this experiment, you are going to place your grid on the floor and hold a centimeter cube about 2 feet above the grid. Without aiming, you will let it drop onto the grid. You will then record the color of the square on which the cube finally lands.

   ◆ If the cube does not land on the grid, the drop does not count.

   ◆ If the cube lands on more than one color, record the color that is covered by most of the cube. If you cannot tell, the toss does not count.

Making a Prediction

3. On which color is the cube *most likely* to land? _____

4. On which color is it *least likely* to land? _____

5. Suppose you were to drop the cube 100 times. How many times would you expect it to land on each color? Record your predictions below.

Predicted Results of 100 Cube Drops			
Color	Number of Squares	Predicted Results Fraction	Percent
yellow	1	$\frac{1}{100}$	_____ %
red	4		_____ %
green	10		_____ %
blue	35		_____ %
white	50		_____ %
Total	**100**	**1**	**100%**

Statistics, Data Analysis, and Probability 2.2; Statistics, Data Analysis, and Probability 2.1; Number Sense 1.6

LESSON 7·12   A Cube-Drop Experiment *continued*

Doing the Experiment

You and your partner will each drop a centimeter cube onto your own colored grid.

6. One partner drops the cube. The other partner records the color in the grid below by writing a letter in one of the squares. Drop the cube a total of 50 times.

Write
y for yellow,
r for red,
g for green,
b for blue, and
w for white.

7. Then trade roles. Do another 50 drops, and record the results in the other partner's journal.

8. Count the number for each color.

   Write it in the "Number of Drops" column.

   Check that the total is 50.

My Results for 50 Cube Drops		
Color	Number of Drops	Percent
yellow		
red		
green		
blue		
white		
Total	**50**	**100%**

9. When you have finished, fill in the percent column in the table.

   Example: If your cube landed on blue 15 times out of 50 drops, this is the same as 30 times out of 100 drops, or 30% of the time.

LESSON 7·12 Place Value in Whole Numbers

1. Write these numbers in order from least to greatest.

964   9,460   96,400   400,960   94,600

_____

_____

_____

_____

_____

2. A number has

5 in the hundreds place,
7 in the ten-thousands place,
0 in the ones place,
9 in the thousands place, and
8 in the tens place.

Write the number.

_____ _____ , _____ _____ _____

3. Write the greatest number you can make with the following digits:

3   5   0   7   9   2

_____

4. What is the value of the digit 8 in the numerals below?

a. **8**07,941 _____

b. 5**8**3 _____

c. **8**,714 _____

d. **8**6,490 _____

5. Write each number using digits.

a. four hundred eighty-seven thousand, sixty-three

_____

b. fifteen thousand, two hundred ninety-seven

_____

6. I am a 5-digit number.

◆ The digit in the thousands place is the result of dividing 64 by 8.

◆ The digit in the ones place is the result of dividing 63 by 9.

◆ The digit in the ten-thousands place is the result of dividing 54 by 6.

◆ The digit in the tens place is the result of dividing 40 by 5.

◆ The digit in the hundreds place is the result of dividing 33 by 11.

What number am I?

_____ _____ , _____ _____ _____

Number Sense 1.0; Number Sense **1.2**

LESSON 7·12   **Math Boxes**

---

1. Name the shaded area as a fraction and a decimal.

  a. fraction:

  _____

  b. decimal:

  _____

SRB
27 61

---

2. Write $<$, $>$, or $=$ to make each number sentence true.

  a. $\dfrac{3}{8}$ _____ $\dfrac{7}{8}$

  b. $\dfrac{5}{12}$ _____ $\dfrac{5}{6}$

  c. $\dfrac{1}{4}$ _____ $\dfrac{1}{15}$

  d. $\dfrac{500}{1,000}$ _____ $\dfrac{8}{16}$

  e. $\dfrac{6}{7}$ _____ $\dfrac{19}{20}$

SRB
53 54

---

3. Write 6 fractions equivalent to $\dfrac{1}{6}$.

  _____   _____

  _____   _____

  _____   _____

SRB
49–51

---

4. Divide. Use a paper-and-pencil algorithm.

  $\dfrac{769}{15}$ = _____

SRB
22 23
179

---

5. Multiply. Use a paper-and-pencil algorithm.

  _____ = 46 ∗ 206

SRB
18 19

---

6. Compare.

  a. 1 day is _____ times as long as 6 hours.

  b. 6 years is _____ times as long as 2 months.

  c. 3 gallons is _____ times as much as 4 cups.

  d. 8 cm is _____ times as long as 5 mm.

  e. 1 meter is _____ times as long as 10 cm.

SRB
315

LESSON 7·13   **Math Boxes**

---

1. Measure the length and width of your desk to the nearest half-inch. Find its perimeter.

   a. Length = _____ inches

   b. Width = _____ inches

   c. Perimeter = _____ inches

   131

2. Find the area of the figure.

    = 1 square centimeter

   Area = _____ square cm

   133

---

3. If 1 centimeter on a map represents 20 kilometers, then

   a. 8 cm represent _____ km.

   b. 3.5 cm represent _____ km.

   c. _____ cm represent 30 km.

   d. _____ cm represent 50 km.

   e. _____ cm represents 10 km.

   145

4. Tell if each of these is closest to 1 inch, 1 foot, or 1 yard.

   a. the width of a door _____

   b. the width of your ankle _____

   c. the length of your little finger _____

   d. the length of your forearm _____

   130

---

5. Complete.

   a. 26 in. = _____ ft _____ in.

   b. 57 in. = _____ ft _____ in.

   c. 9 ft = _____ yd

   d. 16 ft = _____ yd _____ ft

   e. 8 yd = _____ ft

   129

6. Compare.

   a. 1 day is _____ times as long as 12 hours.

   b. 3 years is _____ times as long as 6 months.

   c. 12 cm is _____ times as long as 2 mm.

   d. 1 m is _____ times as long as 20 cm.

   e. 3 gallons is _____ times as much as 2 cups.

   315

---

1) MG 1.4   2) MG 1.1   3) AF 1.4
4) MR 2.1   5) AF 1.5   6) MR 1.2

LESSON 8·1 Kitchen Layouts and Kitchen Efficiency

Here are four common ways to arrange the appliances in a kitchen:

One wall

L-shaped

U-shaped

Pullman or galley

Pullman kitchens are usually found on passenger trains. **Galleys** are the kitchens on boats and airplanes. The kitchen areas on trains, boats, and airplanes are small. The cooking area is usually lined up against a single wall (a one-wall kitchen) or against two walls with a corridor between them (a Pullman or galley kitchen).

◆ What kind of kitchen layout do you have in your home? Circle one.

One wall   L-shaped   (U-shaped)   Pullman or galley

Kitchen efficiency experts are people who study the ways we use our kitchens. They carry out **time-and-motion** studies to find how long it takes to do some kitchen tasks and how much a person has to move about in order to do them. They want to find the best ways to arrange the stove, the sink, and the refrigerator. In an efficient kitchen, a person should have to do very little walking to move from one appliance to another. However, the appliances should not be too close to each other, because the person would feel cramped.

A bird's-eye sketch is often drawn to see how well the appliances in a kitchen are arranged. The stove, the sink, and the refrigerator are connected with line segments as shown below. These segments form a triangle called a **work triangle.** The work triangle shows the distance between pairs of appliances.

Work Triangle

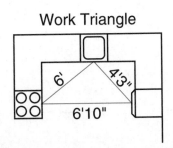

Measurement and Geometry 1.0; Measurement and Geometry 1.4

LESSON 8·1   Layout of My Kitchen

1. Copy the distances between your appliances from *Math Masters*, page 235.

Between stove and refrigerator: About _____8_____ feet _____0_____ inches

Between refrigerator and sink: *largest* → About _____9_____ feet _____52_____ inches

Between sink and stove: *smallest* → About _____24_____ feet _____3_____ inches

2. Cut out the sketch of your kitchen from *Math Masters*, page 236 and tape it in the space below.

$$6+4=19$$
$$0+2+3=5$$
$$\overline{24}$$

Measurement and Geometry 1.0; Measurement and Geometry 1.4

LESSON 8·1   # How Efficient Is My Kitchen?

Answer the questions below to see how well the appliances in your kitchen are arranged.

1. With a straightedge, draw a triangle connecting the appliances in your sketch on page 220. Write the distances between the appliances on the sides of your triangle. This triangle is called a **work triangle.**

2. Find the **perimeter** of your work triangle. Show your work.

_____6_____ feet _____0_____ inches

_____9_____ feet _____2_____ inches

+ _____4_____ feet _____34_____ inches

_____19_____   _____5_____

The perimeter is about _____19____ feet _____5____ inches.

That's close to _____24____ feet.

3. Kitchen efficiency experts recommend the following distances between appliances:

   Between stove and refrigerator: 4 feet to 9 feet

   Between refrigerator and sink: 4 feet to 7 feet

   Between sink and stove: 4 feet to 6 feet

   Does your kitchen meet these recommendations? _____no_____

4. How many students reported their work triangle perimeters? _____13_____ students

   The minimum perimeter is about _____13_____ feet.

   The maximum perimeter is about _____34_____ feet.

   The mode of the perimeters is about _____15_____ feet.

   The median perimeter is about _____20,21_____ feet.

LESSON 8·1 Work Triangles

1. **a.** Below, draw a work triangle that meets all of the following conditions:

   ◆ The perimeter is 21 feet.

   ◆ The length of each side is a whole number of feet.

   ◆ The length of each side is in the recommended range:

Between stove and refrigerator:	4 feet to 9 feet
Between refrigerator and sink:	4 feet to 7 feet
Between sink and stove:	4 feet to 6 feet

   b. Write the distances on the sides of your triangle.

   c. Label each vertex (corner) of the triangle as *stove*, *sink*, or *refrigerator*.

2. Below, draw a different work triangle that meets the same conditions listed in Problem 1.

Measurement and Geometry 1.0; Measurement and Geometry 1.4

LESSON 8·1

Math Boxes

1. Some fourth graders were asked how many minutes they spend studying at home per week. Here are the responses from ten students:

130, 45, 240, 35, 160, 185, 120, 20, 55, 160

a. What is the mode? _____ minutes

b. What is the median? _____ minutes

2. Insert >, <, or = to make each number sentence true.

a. $\dfrac{11}{12}$ _____ $\dfrac{19}{20}$

b. $\dfrac{1}{4}$ _____ $\dfrac{1}{9}$

c. $\dfrac{4}{9}$ _____ $\dfrac{12}{27}$

d. $\dfrac{10}{12}$ _____ $\dfrac{30}{36}$

e. $\dfrac{7}{2}$ _____ $\dfrac{21}{6}$

3. a. Use your Geometry Template to draw an equilateral triangle.

b. Measure one of the angles with your protractor. Record the measure.

_____ °

4. If you spin the spinner below 100 times, how many times would you expect it to land

on red? _____ times

on black? _____ times

on white? _____ times

5. Solve the open sentence $\dfrac{1}{4} + y = \dfrac{3}{8}$. Circle the best answer.

A $y = \dfrac{2}{4}$

B $y = \dfrac{4}{12}$

C $y = \dfrac{1}{8}$

D $y = \dfrac{1}{4}$

6. A store is giving a 50% discount on all merchandise. Find the discounted prices.

Regular price	Discounted price
$26.00	_____
$0.48	_____
$140.60	_____
$65.24	_____

LESSON 8·2 A Floor Plan of My Classroom

When architects design a room or house, they usually make two drawings. The first drawing is called a **rough floor plan.** It is not carefully drawn. But the rough floor plan includes all of the information that is needed to make an accurate drawing. The second drawing is called a **scale drawing.** It is drawn on a grid and is very accurate.

Rough floor plan for a bedroom

Scale drawing for a bedroom
(1 grid length represents 1 foot.)

1. What information do you need to draw a rough floor plan?

   Windows, bookself, walls, doors, cubbies,
   desk, air conditioning, length of desk, and
   shape of room.

Architects use these symbols
to show windows and doors:

window   door opening to left   door opening to right

2. Make a rough floor plan of your classroom in the space below.

Measurement and Geometry 1.0; Measurement and Geometry 1.1

LESSON 8·2   A Floor Plan of My Classroom *continued*

3. Make a scale drawing of your classroom. Scale: _____ inch represents _____ foot.

Each side of a small square in the grid below is $\frac{1}{4}$ inch long.

For use in Lesson 8-3: The area of my classroom is about _____ square feet.

Measurement and Geometry 1.0; Measurement and Geometry 1.1

LESSON 8·2 Math Boxes

1. Measure the sides of the figure to the nearest centimeter. Then find its perimeter.

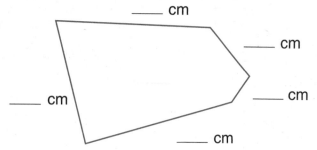

_____ cm

_____ cm

_____ cm

_____ cm

_____ cm

Perimeter = _____ cm

 SRB 131

2. If you tossed a coin onto the grid below, about what fraction of the time would you expect it to land on R?

_____

R	O	P	E
O	P	E	R
P	E	R	O
E	R	O	P

SRB 45 84

3. Write an equivalent fraction, decimal, or whole number.

Decimal	Fraction
a. 0.8	_____
b. _____	$\frac{65}{100}$
c. _____	$\frac{15}{15}$
d. 0.90	_____

SRB 61

4. Which number is closest to the product of 510 and 18? Circle the best answer.

A 100

B 1,000

C 10,000

D 100,000

 SRB 181

5. Write each number in exponential notation.

a. 100 = _____

b. 10,000 = _____

c. 1,000,000 = _____

d. 1,000 = _____

 SRB 5

6. Shade more than $\frac{2}{100}$ but less than $\frac{1}{10}$ of the grid.

 SRB 27

1) MG 1.0   2) SDAP 2.2   3) NS 1.6
4) MR 2.1   5) AF 1.0   6) NS 1.7

Date _____ Time _____

Find the area of each polygon.

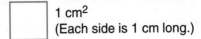 1 cm²
(Each side is 1 cm long.)

SRB
134

1.

Area = ___5___ cm²

2.

Area = ___10___ cm²

3.

Area = ___9___ cm²

4.

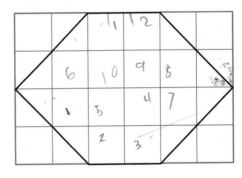

Area = ___16___ cm²

5.

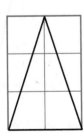

Area = ___3___ cm²

6.

Area = ___8___ cm²

7.

Area = ___6___ cm²

LESSON 8·3 Math Boxes

---

1. Use the set of numbers 8, 20, 17, 16, 5, 15, and 9 to answer the questions.

What is the

a. maximum? _____

b. minimum? _____

c. range? _____

d. median? _____

SRB 73

---

2. Insert >, <, or = to make each number sentence true.

a. $\frac{1}{15}$ _____ $\frac{1}{6}$

b. $\frac{2}{3}$ _____ $\frac{4}{3}$

c. $\frac{4}{8}$ _____ $\frac{7}{15}$

d. $\frac{12}{18}$ _____ $\frac{4}{6}$

e. $\frac{7}{8}$ _____ $\frac{49}{50}$

SRB 53 54

---

3. a. Use your Geometry Template to draw a regular hexagon.

b. Measure one of the angles with your protractor. Record the measure.

_____ °

SRB 97 142 143

---

4. If you spin the spinner below 800 times, how many times would you expect it to land

on red? _____ times

on black? _____ times

on white? _____ times

on blue? _____ times

SRB 84

---

5. Add or subtract.

a. $\frac{3}{10} + x = \frac{4}{10}$ $x =$ _____

b. $m + \frac{2}{3} = \frac{5}{6}$ $m =$ _____

c. $s - \frac{4}{9} = \frac{3}{9}$ $s =$ _____

d. $\frac{7}{8} - t = \frac{3}{4}$ $t =$ _____

SRB 55 57

---

6. A store is giving a 50% discount on all merchandise. Find the discounted prices.

Regular price	Discounted price
$0.80	_____
$22.00	_____
$24.68	_____
$124.70	_____

SRB 38 39

---

1) SDAP 1.2 2) AF 1.0 3) MG 3.0
4) SDAP 2.2 5) AF 2.1 6) AF 2.2

LESSON
8·4

Math Boxes

---

1. Measure the sides of the figure to the nearest centimeter. Then find its perimeter.

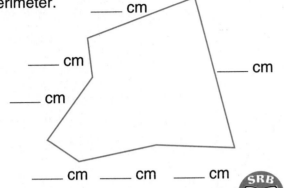

_____ cm

_____ cm   _____ cm

_____ cm

_____ cm _____ cm _____ cm

Perimeter = _____ cm

SRB 131

---

2. If you tossed a coin onto the grid below, about what fraction of the time would you expect it to land on a vowel?

_____

R	O	P	E
O	P	E	R
P	E	R	O
E	R	O	P

SRB 45 84

---

3. Write an equivalent fraction, decimal, or whole number.

	Decimal	Fraction
a.	0.1	_____
b.	0.20	_____
c.	_____	$\frac{4}{5}$
d.	_____	$\frac{0}{3}$

SRB 61

---

4. Which number is closest to the product of 192 and 49? Circle the best answer.

A 100

B 1,000

C 10,000

D 100,000

SRB 181

---

5. Write each number in exponential notation.

a. 100,000 = _____

b. 10 = _____

c. 10,000,000 = _____

d. 1,000,000,000 = _____

SRB 5

---

6. Shade more than $\frac{18}{100}$ but less than $\frac{3}{10}$ of the grid.

SRB 27

LESSON 8·4
What Is the Total Area of My Skin?

Follow your teacher's directions to complete this page.

1. There are _____ square inches in 1 square foot.

1 ft

1 square foot

2. My guess is that the total
   area of my skin is about _____ square feet.

> *Rule of Thumb:* The total area of your skin is about
> 100 times the area of the outline of your hand.

Follow these steps to estimate the total area of your skin:

- ◆ Ask your partner to trace the outline of your hand on the grid on page 231.

- ◆ Estimate the area of the outline of your hand by counting squares on the grid.
  Record your estimate in Problem 3 below.

- ◆ Use the rule of thumb to estimate the total area of your skin (area of skin =
  100 * area of hand). Record your estimate in Problem 4 below.

3. I estimate that the area of the outline of my hand is about _____ square inches.

4. I estimate that the total area of my skin is about _____ square inches.

5. I estimate that the total area of my skin is about _____ square feet.

6. a. There are _____ square feet
      in 1 square yard.

   b. I estimate that the total area of my
      skin is about _____ square yards.

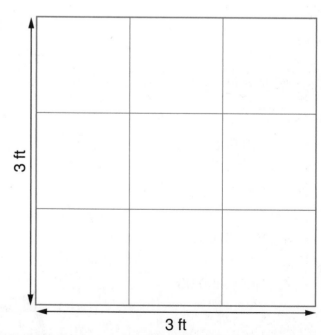

3 ft

3 ft

1 square yard

Measurement and Geometry 1.0, 1.1; Mathematical Reasoning 2.2, 2.5

LESSON 8·4 What Is the Total Area of My Skin? *continued*

Ask your partner to trace the outline of your hand onto the grid below.
Keep your 4 fingers and thumb together.

Each grid square has 1-inch sides and an area of 1 square inch.

LESSON 8·5

Areas of Rectangles

Math Message

1. Find the area of each rectangle.

1 cm²

A

B

C

Area = ____8____ cm²   Area = ____9____ cm²   Area = ____30____ cm²

2. Fill in the table.

Rectangle	Number of squares per row	Number of rows	Total number of squares	Number model
A	4	2	8	2 * 4 = 8
B	3	3	9	3 * 3 = 9
C	5	6	30	6 X 5 = 30

3. Write a formula for the area of a rectangle.

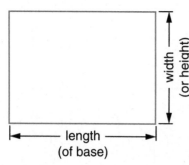

width (or height)

length (of base)

Area = ___l x w___

b x h

Measurement and Geometry 1.1, 1.4; Algebra and Functions 1.1, 1.4; Mathematical Reasoning 1.1

Date _____   Time _____

Areas of Rectangles *continued*

4. Fill in the table at the bottom of the page.

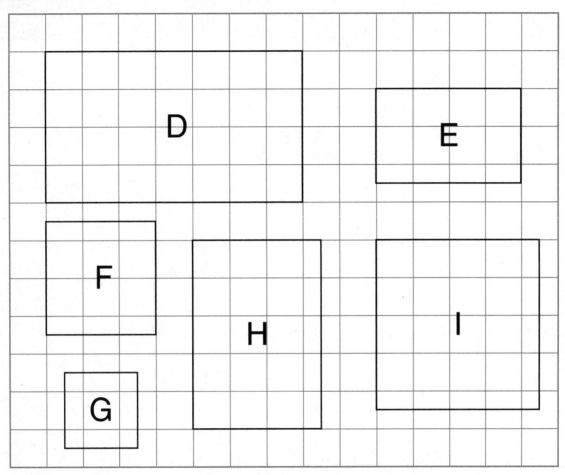

Rectangle	Area (counting squares)	Length (of base)	Width (or height)	Area (using formula)
D	_____ cm²	_____ cm	_____ cm	_____ cm²
E	_____ cm²	_____ cm	_____ cm	_____ cm²
F	_____ cm²	_____ cm	_____ cm	_____ cm²
G	_____ cm²	_____ cm	_____ cm	_____ cm²
H	_____ cm²	_____ cm	_____ cm	_____ cm²
I	_____ cm²	_____ cm	_____ cm	_____ cm²

LESSON
8·5

Coordinate Grids

1. Plot and label each point on the coordinate grid.

A   (2,6)

B   (5,5)

C   (8,3)

D   (4,2)

E   (8,9)

F   (2,10)

G   (5,8)

H   (1,4)

2. Write the ordered number pair for each point plotted on the coordinate grid.

I   (_____ , _____)

J   (_____ , _____)

K   (_____ , _____)

L   (_____ , _____)

M (_____ , _____)

N   (_____ , _____)

O   (_____ , _____)

P   (_____ , _____)

Q   (_____ , _____)

R   (_____ , _____)

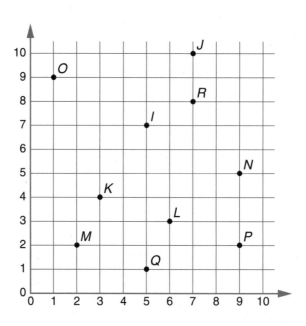

Measurement and Geometry **2.0**; Measurement and Geometry **2.2**; Measurement and Geometry **2.3**

LESSON 8·5 **Math Boxes**

---

1. Write three equivalent fractions for each fraction.

a. $\frac{1}{2}$ _____, _____, _____

b. $\frac{3}{4}$ _____, _____, _____

c. $\frac{2}{3}$ _____, _____, _____

d. $\frac{5}{6}$ _____, _____, _____

SRB 49–51

---

2. Find the perimeter of this polygon.

Number model:

_____

_____

Perimeter = _____ cm

---

3. Complete the "What's My Rule?" table, and state the rule.

Rule: _____

in	out
3.66	7.02
0.44	3.80
8.73	
	12.66

SRB 162–166

---

4. If you throw a die 60 times, about how many times would you expect to come up?

_____ times

SRB 81

---

5. Complete.

a. _____ is half as much as 44.

b. 90 is twice as much as _____.

c. _____ is 3 times as much as 40.

d. 20 is $\frac{1}{5}$ of _____.

e. _____ is 5 times as much as 34.

---

6. Divide with a paper-and-pencil algorithm.

5,682 / 4 = _____

SRB 22 23 179

LESSON 8·6 Areas of Parallelograms

SRB
135

1. Cut out Parallelogram A on *Math Masters,* page 260.
   DO NOT CUT OUT THE ONE BELOW. Cut it into
   2 pieces so that it can be made into a rectangle.

1 cm²

Parallelogram A

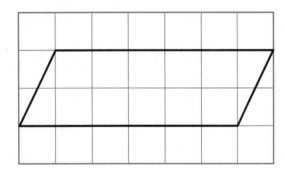

Tape your rectangle in the space below.

base = _____ cm

length of base = _____ cm

height = _____ cm

width (height) = _____ cm

Area of parallelogram = _____ cm²

Area of rectangle = _____ cm²

2. Do the same with Parallelogram B on *Math Masters,* page 260.

Parallelogram B

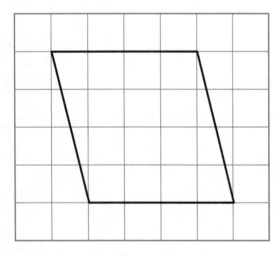

Tape your rectangle in the space below.

base = _____ cm

length of base = _____ cm

height = _____ cm

width (height) = _____ cm

Area of parallelogram = _____ cm²

Area of rectangle = _____ cm²

Measurement and Geometry 1.4; Algebra and Functions 1.1; Algebra and Functions 1.4

LESSON 8·6   **Areas of Parallelograms** *continued*

3. Do the same with Parallelogram C.

Parallelogram C

Tape your rectangle in the space below.

base = _____ cm

height = _____ cm

Area of parallelogram = _____ cm²

length of base = _____ cm

width (height) = _____ cm

Area of rectangle = _____ cm²

---

4. Do the same with Parallelogram D.

Parallelogram D

Tape your rectangle in the space below.

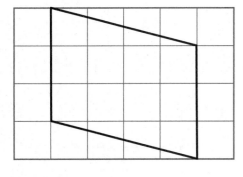

base = _____ cm

height = _____ cm

Area of parallelogram = _____ cm²

length of base = _____ cm

width (height) = _____ cm

Area of rectangle = _____ cm²

---

5. Write a formula for the area of a parallelogram.

_____

LESSON 8·6 **Areas of Parallelograms** *continued*

6. Draw a line segment to show the height of Parallelogram *DORA*.

   Use your ruler to measure the base and height.
   Then find the area.

   base = _____ cm

   height = _____ cm

   Area = _____ cm²

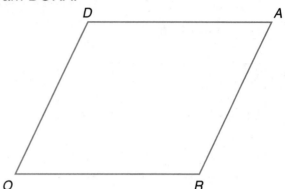

7. Draw the following shapes on the grid below:

   a. A rectangle whose area is 12 square centimeters

   b. A parallelogram, not a rectangle, whose area is 12 square centimeters

   c. A different parallelogram whose area is also 12 square centimeters

8. What is the area of:

   a. Parallelogram *ABCD*?   b. Trapezoid *EBCD*?   c. Triangle *ABE*?

   _____ cm²   _____ cm²   _____ cm²

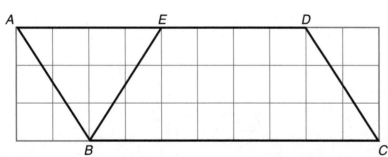

Measurement and Geometry 1.4; Algebra and Functions 1.1; Algebra and Functions 1.4

LESSON 8·6 Math Boxes

1. Dimensions for actual rectangles are given. Make scale drawings of each rectangle described below.

Scale: 1 cm represents 20 meters.

a. Length of rectangle: 80 meters
Width of rectangle: 30 meters

b. Length of rectangle: 90 meters
Width of rectangle: 50 meters

SRB
145

---

2. What is the area of the parallelogram?

Number model: _____

Area = _____ in²

SRB
135

---

3. A jar contains

8 blue blocks,

4 red blocks,

9 orange blocks, and

4 green blocks.

You put your hand in the jar and without looking pull out a block. About what fraction of the time would you expect to get a blue block?

_____

SRB
45

---

4. Add or subtract.

a. $\frac{3}{16} + \frac{7}{16} =$ _____

b. $\frac{2}{3} + \frac{1}{6} =$ _____

c. _____ $= \frac{9}{10} - \frac{3}{10}$

d. _____ $= \frac{3}{4} - \frac{3}{8}$

SRB
55 57

---

5. Multiply. Use a paper-and-pencil algorithm.

_____ = 83 * 74

SRB
18 19

LESSON 8·7 Areas of Triangles

1. Cut out Triangles A and B from *Math Masters,* page 265.
   DO NOT CUT OUT THE ONE BELOW. Tape the two triangles
   together to form a parallelogram.

1 cm²

Triangle A

Tape your parallelogram in the space below.

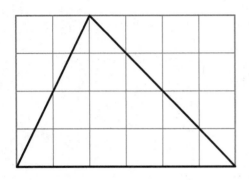

base = _____ cm   base = _____ cm

height = _____ cm   height = _____ cm

Area of triangle = _____ cm²   Area of parallelogram = _____ cm²

2. Do the same with Triangles C and D on *Math Masters,* page 265.

Triangle C

Tape your parallelogram in the space below.

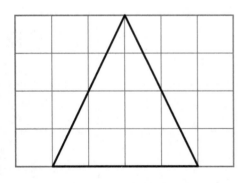

base = _____ cm   base = _____ cm

height = _____ cm   height = _____ cm

Area of triangle = _____ cm²   Area of parallelogram = _____ cm²

Measurement and Geometry 1.4; Algebra and Functions 1.1; Algebra and Functions 1.4

LESSON 8·7 **Areas of Triangles** *continued*

3. Do the same with Triangles E and F.

Triangle E

Tape your parallelogram in the space below.

base = _____ cm

base = _____ cm

height = _____ cm

height = _____ cm

Area of triangle = _____ cm²

Area of parallelogram = _____ cm²

4. Do the same with Triangles G and H.

Triangle G

Tape your parallelogram in the space below.

base = _____ cm

base = _____ cm

height = _____ cm

height = _____ cm

Area of triangle = _____ cm²

Area of parallelogram = _____ cm²

5. Write a formula for the area of a triangle.

_____

height

length of base

LESSON 8·7 **Areas of Triangles** *continued*

6. Draw a line segment to show the height of Triangle *SAM*.
   Use your ruler to measure the base and height of the
   triangle. Then find the area.

   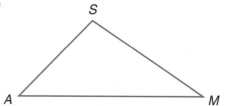

   base = _____ cm

   height = _____ cm

   Area = _____ cm²

7. Draw three *different* triangles on the grid below. Each triangle must have
   an area of 3 square centimeters. One triangle should have a right angle.

   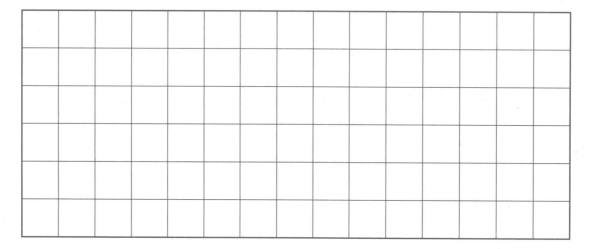

8. See the shapes below. Which has the larger area—the star or the square? Explain your answer.

   _____

   _____

   _____

Measurement and Geometry 1.4; Algebra and Functions 1.1, 1.2, 1.4; Mathematical Reasonings 2.3

Date _____   Time _____

1. Circle $\frac{1}{6}$ of the triangles. Mark Xs on $\frac{2}{3}$ of the triangles.

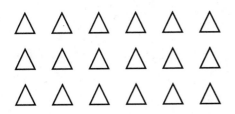

2. **a.** Shade $\frac{2}{5}$ of the pentagon.

b. Shade $\frac{3}{5}$ of the pentagon.

3. There are 56 musicians in the school band: $\frac{1}{4}$ of the musicians play the flute and $\frac{1}{8}$ play the trombone.

   a. How many musicians play the flute? _____

   b. How many musicians play the trombone? _____

4. Wei had 48 bean-bag animals in her collection. She sold 18 of them to another collector. What fraction of her collection did she sell?

   _____

5. Complete.

   a. $\frac{3}{4}$ of _____ is 90.

   b. _____ of 27 is 18.

   c. $\frac{5}{6}$ of 120 is _____.

   d. $\frac{3}{10}$ of _____ is 15.

   e. _____ of 72 is 24.

   f. $\frac{5}{4}$ of 16 is _____.

6. Fill in the missing fractions on the number line.

LESSON 8·7

Math Boxes

1. Write three equivalent fractions for each fraction.

a. $\frac{4}{9}$ _____ , _____ , _____

b. $\frac{3}{8}$ _____ , _____ , _____

c. $\frac{2}{5}$ _____ , _____ , _____

d. $\frac{7}{10}$ _____ , _____ , _____

SRB 49–51

2. Measure the sides of the figure to the nearest centimeter to find its perimeter.

Perimeter = _____ cm

SRB 131

3. Complete the "What's My Rule?" table, and state the rule.

Rule: _____

in	out
8.69	4.09
11.03	6.43
	15.34
26.05	

SRB 162–166

4. If you throw a die 420 times, about how many times would you expect to come up? Circle the best answer.

A 70 times

B 100 times

C 50 times

D 210 times

SRB 81

5. Complete.

a. _____ is half as much as 86.

b. 48 is twice as much as _____ .

c. _____ is 3 times as much as 50.

d. 40 is $\frac{1}{5}$ of _____ .

e. _____ is 5 times as much as 27.

6. Divide with a paper-and-pencil algorithm.

7,653 / 6 = _____

SRB 22 23 179

1) NS 1.5   2) MG 1.4   3) NS 2.0
4) SDAP 2.2   5) AF 2.0   6) NS 3.2

LESSON 8·8   Comparing Country Areas

Brazil is the largest country in South America. Brazil's area is about 3,300,000 square miles. The area of the United States is about 3,500,000 square miles. So Brazil is nearly the same size as the United States.

Fill in the table below. This will help you to compare the areas of other countries in South America to Brazil's area. Round quotients in Part 4 to the nearest tenth.

Country	(1) Guess the number of times it would fit in the area of Brazil.	(2) Area	(3) Area (rounded to the nearest 10,000)	(4) Divide the rounded areas. (Brazil area ÷ country area)
Ecuador	_____	109,500 mi^2	_____ mi^2	3,300,000 ÷ _____ = _____
Argentina	_____	1,068,300 mi^2	_____ mi^2	3,300,000 ÷ _____ = _____
Paraguay	_____	157,000 mi^2	_____ mi^2	3,300,000 ÷ _____ = _____
Peru	_____	496,200 mi^2	_____ mi^2	3,300,000 ÷ _____ = _____
Uruguay	_____	68,000 mi^2	_____ mi^2	3,300,000 ÷ _____ = _____
Chile	_____	292,300 mi^2	_____ mi^2	3,300,000 ÷ _____ = _____

Number Sense **1.3**; Measurement and Geometry 1.0

245

LESSON 8·8 **Math Boxes**

1. Make scale drawings of each rectangle described below.

Scale: 1 cm represents 1.5 meters.

a. Length of rectangle: 6 meters
Width of rectangle: 3 meters

b. Length of rectangle: 10.5 meters
Width of rectangle: 4.5 meters

SRB
145

---

2. What is the area of the parallelogram?

8"

1"

Number model: _____

Area = _____ in²

SRB
135

---

3. A jar contains

27 blue blocks,

18 red blocks,

12 orange blocks, and

43 green blocks.

You put your hand in the jar and without looking pull out a block. About what fraction of the time would you expect to get a red block?

_____

SRB
45

---

4. Add or subtract.

a. $\frac{1}{12} + \frac{11}{12} =$ _____

b. $\frac{1}{6} + \frac{2}{3} =$ _____

c. _____ $= \frac{7}{8} - \frac{5}{8}$

d. _____ $= \frac{5}{16} - \frac{1}{8}$

SRB
55 57

---

5. Multiply. Use a paper-and-pencil algorithm.

91 * 48 = _____

SRB
18 19

1) MR 2.3   2) MG 1.4   3) SDAP 2.2
4) MR 2.0   5) NS 3.2

LESSON 8·9   **Math Boxes**

1. A store is giving a 50% discount on all merchandise. Find the discounted prices.

Regular price	Discounted price
$53.00	_____
$0.96	_____
$111.10	_____
$75.50	_____

2. Shade more than $\frac{70}{100}$ but less than $\frac{9}{10}$ of the grid.

3. Multiply. Use a paper-and-pencil algorithm.

   a. $482 * 6 =$ _____
   b. $75 * 84 =$ _____
   c. $36 * 58 =$ _____

4. Divide. Use a paper-and-pencil algorithm.

   a. $853 / 7 =$ _____
   b. $7,342 \div 5 =$ _____
   c. $\dfrac{385}{12} =$ _____

LESSON 9·1 **Many Names for Percents**

Your teacher will tell you how to fill in the percent examples.

Fill in the "100% box" for each example. Show the percent by shading the 10-by-10 grid. Then write other names for the percent next to the grid.

Example: Last season, Duncan made 62 percent of his basketball shots.

100%

all of Duncan's shots

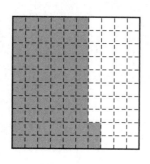

That is __62__ out of every 100.

Fraction name: $\frac{62}{100}$

Decimal name: _0.62_

---

1. Percent Example: _____

_____

_____

100%

That is _____ out of every 100.

Fraction name: $\frac{}{100}$

Decimal name: _____

---

2. Percent Example: _____

_____

_____

100%

That is _____ out of every 100.

Fraction name: $\frac{}{100}$

Decimal name: _____

Number Sense 1.6; Number Sense 1.7

LESSON 9·1 Many Names for Percents *continued*

Fill in the "100% box" for each example. (Problem 3 is done for you.)
Show the percent by shading the 10-by-10 grid. Then write other names
for the percent next to the grid.

3. Example: 12% of the students in Marshall School are left-handed.

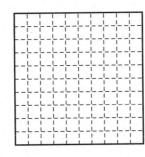

100%

*all students at
Marshall School*

That is _____ out of every 100.

Fraction name: $\dfrac{\boxed{}}{100}$

Decimal name: _____

4. Example: Sarah spelled 80% of the words correctly on her last test.

100%

That is _____ out of every 100.

Fraction name: $\dfrac{\boxed{}}{100}$

Decimal name: _____

5. Example: Cats sleep about 58% of the time.

100%

That is _____ out of every 100.

Fraction name: $\dfrac{\boxed{}}{100}$

Decimal name: _____

LESSON 9·1   Many Names for Percents *continued*

Fill in the "100% box" for each example. Show the percent by shading
the 10-by-10 grid. Write other names for the percent next to the grid.
Then answer the question.

6. Example: *Sale—40% Off*
Everything Must Go!

100%

That is _____ out of every 100.

Fraction name: $\dfrac{\boxed{}}{100}$

Decimal name: _____

What would Mr. Thompson pay for a bicycle that had been selling for $300? _____

7. Example: A carpet store ran a TV commercial that said:
"Pay 20% when you order. Take 1 full year to pay the rest."

100%

That is _____ out of every 100.

Fraction name: $\dfrac{\boxed{}}{100}$

Decimal name: _____

Mrs. Shields wants to order a $1,200 carpet. How much must she pay

when she orders it? _____

Number Sense 1.6; Number Sense 1.7

LESSON 9·1 Math Boxes

1. In which situation below do you need to know the area? Choose the best answer.

- ⊂⊃ finding the distance around a pool
- ⊂⊃ buying a wallpaper border for your bedroom
- ⊂⊃ carpeting the living room
- ⊂⊃ fencing a yard

2. Complete.

Rule:

_____

in	out
$\frac{2}{5}$	$\frac{3}{5}$
$\frac{1}{10}$	$\frac{3}{10}$
$\frac{4}{5}$	
	$\frac{9}{10}$
	$\frac{1}{2}$

3. Multiply. Use a paper-and-pencil algorithm.

_____ = 58 * 76

4. Find the approximate latitude and longitude of these Region 2 cities.

a. Dublin, Ireland latitude _____ ° _____

longitude _____ ° _____

b. Rome, Italy latitude _____ ° _____

longitude _____ ° _____

5. Angle *RST* is an _____ (acute or obtuse) angle.

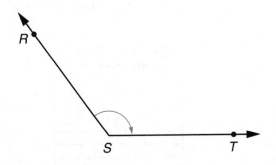

The measure of ∠ *RST* is _____ °.

6. Use a straightedge to draw the line of symmetry.

LESSON 9·2 **"Percent-of" Number Stories**

Alfred, Nadine, Kyla, and Jackson each took the same math test. There were 20 problems on the test.

100%

20-problem test

1. Alfred missed $\frac{1}{2}$ of the problems. He missed 0.50 of the problems. That is 50% of the problems.

   How many problems did he miss? _____ problems

   $\frac{1}{2}$ of 20 = _____

   50% of 20 = _____

$\frac{1}{2}$, or 50% is shaded.

2. Nadine missed $\frac{1}{4}$ of the problems. She missed 0.25 of the problems. That is 25% of the problems.

   How many problems did she miss? _____ problems

   $\frac{1}{4}$ of 20 = _____

   25% of 20 = _____

$\frac{1}{4}$, or 25% is shaded.

3. Kyla missed $\frac{1}{10}$ of the problems. She missed 0.10 of the problems. That is 10% of the problems.

   How many problems did she miss? _____ problems

   $\frac{1}{10}$ of 20 = _____

   10% of 20 = _____

$\frac{1}{10}$, or 10% is shaded.

4. Jackson missed $\frac{1}{5}$ of the problems. He missed 0.20 of the problems. That is 20% of the problems.

   How many problems did he miss? _____ problems

   $\frac{1}{5}$ of 20 = _____

   20% of 20 = _____

$\frac{1}{5}$, or 20% is shaded.

Number Sense 1.5

Fractions, Decimals, and Percents

Fill in the missing numbers.
Problem 1 has been done
for you.

100%

large square

1. Ways of showing $\frac{3}{4}$:

$\frac{3}{4}$ is shaded. $\frac{75}{100}$

0.__75__   __75__%

2. Ways of showing $\frac{2}{5}$:

$\frac{2}{5}$ is shaded. $\frac{40}{100}$

0.__40__   __40__%

3. Ways of showing $\frac{3}{5}$:

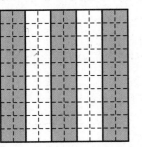

$\frac{3}{5}$ is shaded. $\frac{60}{100}$

0.__60__   __60__%

4. Ways of showing $\frac{4}{5}$:

$\frac{4}{5}$ is shaded. $\frac{80}{100}$

0.__80__   __90__%

5. Ways of showing $\frac{5}{5}$:

$\frac{5}{5}$ is shaded. $\frac{100}{100}$

1.0   100%

Shade the grid. Then fill in the missing numbers.

6. Ways of showing $\frac{3}{10}$:

$\frac{30}{100}$ is shaded.

0.__30__   __30__%

7. Ways of showing $\frac{7}{10}$:

$\frac{70}{100}$ is shaded.

0.__70__   __70__%

8. Ways of showing $\frac{9}{10}$:

$\frac{90}{100}$ is shaded.

0.__90__   __90__%

LESSON 9·2 **Math Boxes**

1. Complete the table with equivalent names.

Fraction	Decimal	Percent
$\frac{1}{5}$		
	0.80	
$\frac{3}{10}$		
		90%

SRB
61 62

2. About 4.02% of the words on the Internet are *the,* and about 1.68% of the words are *and.* About what percent of all words on the Internet are either *the* or *and?* Choose the best answer.

- ⬭ 5.71%

- ⬭ 5.7%

- ⬭ 570%

- ⬭ 57%

SRB
34–37

3. Complete.

a. 3 yd 2 ft = _____ ft

b. 6 yd 1 ft = _____ ft

c. _____ in. = 2 yd

d. _____ ft = 5 yd 2 ft

e. 25 ft = _____ yd _____ ft

f. _____ ft _____ in. = 30 in.

SRB
129

4. Zena earned $12. She spent $8.

a. What fraction of her earnings did she spend? _____

b. What fraction did she have left? _____

c. The amount she spent is how many times as much as the amount she saved?

_____

SRB
44

5. Find the area and perimeter of the rectangle. Include the correct units.

7"

4"

Area = _____

Perimeter = _____

SRB
131 133

6. What temperature is it?

_____°F

SRB
139

1) NS 1.6   2) NS 2.1   3) AF 1.5
4) MR 3.3   5) MG 1.4   6) NS 1.8

LESSON 9·3   **Math Boxes**

---

1. Write A or P to tell whether you would need to find the area or the perimeter in each situation.

a. buying a garden fence _____

b. finding the square footage of your bedroom _____

c. buying wallpaper for the kitchen _____

SRB 131 133

---

2. Complete.

Rule:

_____

in	out
$\frac{7}{9}$	$\frac{4}{9}$
	$\frac{1}{9}$
$\frac{9}{18}$	
$\frac{6}{9}$	$\frac{1}{3}$

SRB 162–166

---

3. Multiply. Use a paper-and-pencil algorithm.

_____ = 64 * 23

SRB 18 19

---

4. Find the approximate latitude and longitude of these Region 4 cities.

a. Calcutta, India latitude _____ ° _____

longitude _____ ° _____

b. Seoul, Korea latitude _____ ° _____

longitude _____ ° _____

SRB 272 273

---

5. Angle *RLA* is an _____ (acute or obtuse) angle.

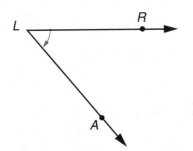

The measure of ∠*RLA* is _____ °.

SRB 141–143

---

6. Use a straightedge to draw the line of symmetry.

SRB 109

LESSON 9·4   Discount Number Stories

1. A store is offering a **discount** of 10% on all items. This means that you save $\frac{1}{10}$ of the **regular price.** Find the sale price of each item below. The **sale price** is the amount you pay after subtracting the discount from the regular price.

Item	Regular Price	Discount (10% of regular price)	Sale Price (Subtract: regular price – discount)
CD player	$140	$14	
Giant screen TV	$1,200		
Radio	$80		
DVD player		$3	

2. Use a drawing and number models to explain how you found the discount and sale price for the radio.

_____

_____

3. An airline offers a 25% discount on the regular airfare for tickets purchased at least 1 month in advance. Find the sale price of each ticket below.

Regular Airfare	Discount (25% of regular airfare)	Sale Price (Subtract: regular airfare – discount)
$400	$100	
$240		
	$75	

4. Use a drawing and number models to explain how you found the regular airfare when you knew $75 was 25% of the regular airfare.

_____

_____

Number Sense 1.6; Mathematical Reasoning 2.3

LESSON 9·4   Discount Number Stories *continued*

5. The regular price of a swing set is $400. Mrs. Lefevre received a
   30% discount because she ordered it during the Big Spring Sale.

   a. How much did she save? _____

   b. How much did she pay? _____

   c. Explain how you solved the problem.

   _____

   _____

   _____

Try This

6. You can pay for a refrigerator by making 12 payments of $50 each.
   Or you can save 25% if you pay for it all at once.

   a. How much will the refrigerator cost if you pay for it all at once? _____

   b. Explain how you solved the problem.

   _____

   _____

   _____

7. Write your own discount number story. Ask a partner to solve it.

   _____

   _____

   _____

LESSON 9·4

Cellular Telephone Use

1. Use the "Subscriptions per 100 People" data in the Cellular Telephone Use table at the bottom of *Student Reference Book,* page 302 to complete the bar graph. Round each decimal to the nearest whole number.

Cellular Telephone Use

Subscriptions per 100 People

112
110
108
106
104
102
100
98
96
94
92
90

Taiwan   Luxembourg   Italy   Iceland   Israel   Spain

Countries

2. Write a question that can be answered by looking at the data displayed in the bar graph. Answer the question.

_____

_____

_____

LESSON 9·4 **Math Boxes**

1. Complete the table with equivalent names.

Fraction	Decimal	Percent
$\frac{3}{4}$		
	0.6	
$\frac{1}{10}$		
		50%

SRB
61 62

2. About 1.96% of the words on the Internet are *a*, and about 0.81% of the words are *it*. What percent of all words on the Internet are either *a* or *it*? Show your work.

_____

SRB
34–37

3. 2 ft 7 in. = __ in. Choose the best answer.

◯ 14

◯ 24

◯ 27

◯ 31

SRB
129

4. Three girls cut a pizza into 12 equal slices and plan to share the pizza equally.

a. What fraction of the pizza should each girl get? _____

b. How many slices should each girl get? _____ slices

c. Suppose 2 more girls arrive. How many slices should each of the 5 girls get?

_____ slices

SRB
44

5. Find the area and perimeter of the rectangle. Include the correct units.

6"

2"

Area = _____

Perimeter = _____

SRB
131 133

6. What temperature is it?

_____°C

SRB
139

LESSON 9·5 **Math Boxes**

1. Calculate.

   a. 10% of 70 = _____

   b. 5% of 60 = _____

   c. 25% of _____ = 7

   d. _____% of 48 = 24

   e. _____% of 25 = 20

   SRB 38 39

2. Insert parentheses to make each number sentence true.

   a. 6 + 2 * 4 = 32

   b. 5 + 7 * 3 = 36

   c. 1 + 8 * 8 + 2 = 90

   d. 1 + 7 * 8 + 2 = 80

   SRB 150

3. Complete the table with equivalent names.

Fraction	Decimal	Percent
$\frac{5}{10}$		
	0.20	
		70%
	0.4	

SRB 61 62

4. Divide. Use a paper-and-pencil algorithm.

897 ÷ 6 = _____

SRB 22 23

5. What is the height of the parallelogram? Include the correct unit.

9 in.

Area = 27 in²

Number model: _____

Height: _____

SRB 135

6. Draw the mirror image of the figure shown on the left of the vertical line.

SRB 106 109

  1) AF 2.2   2) AF 1.3   3) NS 1.6
4) NS 3.2   5) MG 1.4   6) MG 3.4

LESSON 9·6 Trivia Survey Results

1. The chart below will show the results of the trivia survey for the whole class.
   Wait for your teacher to explain how to fill in the chart.

Class Results for the Trivia Survey

Question	Yes	No	Total	$\frac{\text{Yes}}{\text{Total}}$	% Yes
1. Is Monday your favorite day?					
2. Have you gone to the movies in the last month?					
3. Did you eat breakfast today?					
4. Do you keep a map in your car?					
5. Did you eat at a fast-food restaurant yesterday?					
6. Did you read a book during the last month?					
7. Are you more than 1 meter tall?					
8. Do you like liver?					

2. On the basis of the survey results, is it more likely that a person will

   a. read a book or go to a movie?

   _____

   b. eat breakfast or eat at a fast-food restaurant?

   _____

   c. like liver or like Mondays?

   _____

LESSON 9·6 Math Boxes

---

1. If you threw a 6-sided die 54 times, about how many times would you expect it to land on a number less than 3? Choose the best answer.

○ 9 times

○ 12 times

○ 18 times

○ 36 times

2. Name a percent value

a. greater than $\frac{1}{4}$ and less than $\frac{2}{3}$.

_____

b. less than $\frac{4}{5}$ and greater than $\frac{5}{8}$.

_____

---

3. Store X is selling bathing suits at 20% off the regular price of $35. Store Y is selling the same suits for $\frac{1}{4}$ off the regular price of $32. Which store is offering the better buy?

_____

Show how you solved the problem.

4. If 1 inch on a map represents 200 miles, then

a. 5 inches represent _____ miles.

b. 8 inches represent _____ miles.

c. _____ inches represent 800 miles.

d. $3\frac{1}{4}$ inches represent _____ miles.

e. _____ inches represent 350 miles.

---

5. What is the area of the triangle? Include the correct unit.

6"

8"

Number model: _____

Area = _____

6. **a.** Which is warmer, −15°C or −3°C?

_____

How many degrees warmer?

_____

b. Which is colder, −15°C or −20°C?

_____

How many degrees colder?

---

1) SDAP 2.0   2) NS 1.9   3) MR 2.3
4) AF 1.4   5) MG 1.4   6) NS 1.8

LESSON 9·7   **Math Boxes**

---

1. Calculate.

 a. 10% of 50 = _____

 b. 5% of 80 = _____

 c. 20% of _____ = 8

 d. _____% of 16 = 12

 e. _____% of 24 = 6

2. Insert parentheses to make each number sentence true.

 a. 63 / 21 − 12 = 7

 b. 34 − 8 + 4 = 22

 c. 3 ∗ 5 + 6 > 3 ∗ 10

 d. 6 ∗ 7 + 1 > (80 / 2) + 5

---

3. Complete the table with equivalent names.

Fraction	Decimal	Percent
		63%
	1.00	
$\frac{3}{5}$		
		80%

4. Divide. Use a paper-and-pencil algorithm.

420 ÷ 16 = _____

---

5. What is the area of the parallelogram? Include the correct unit.

2"

5"

Number model: _____

Area = _____

6. Draw the mirror image of the figure shown on the left of the vertical line.

LESSON 9·7 Color-Coded Population Maps

1. List the countries in Region 4 from *least to greatest* according to the **percent of population, ages 0–14.** Take one copy of *Math Masters,* page 293 and write a title for your first map. Color these countries using the color code shown below.

Rank	Country	Percent of Population Ages 0–14	Color Code
1	Japan	15%	blue
2			blue
3			blue
4			green
5			green
6			green
7			green
8			red
9			red
10	Bangladesh	34%	red

2. List the countries in Region 4 from *least to greatest* according to the **percent of population that is rural.** Take another copy of *Math Masters,* page 293 and write a title for your second map. Color these countries using the color code shown below.

Rank	Country	Percent of Rural Population	Color Code
1			blue
2			blue
3			blue
4			green
5			green
6			green
7			green
8			red
9			red
10			red

Number Sense 1.2; Statistics, Data Analysis, and Probability 1.0

LESSON 9·7   Color-Coded Population Maps continued

3. What do the map colors mean?

   a. blue _____

   b. green _____

   c. red _____

4. a. Which countries are colored blue on both maps?

   _____

   b. What does this tell you about these countries?

   _____

   _____

5. a. Which countries are colored red on both maps?

   _____

   b. What does this tell you about these countries?

   _____

   _____

6. a. Based on the data tables and maps, do you think there is a connection
   between the percent of young people who live in a particular country
   and the percent of people who live in rural areas?   _____

   Explain your answer.

   _____

   _____

   _____

   _____

   _____

   b. How does your conclusion compare with the prediction that you made
   at the beginning of the lesson?

   _____

   _____

**LESSON
9·7**   **Probability**

1. For this spinner, about what fraction of the spins would you expect to land on blue?

_____ of the spins

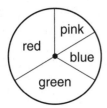

2. Design a spinner so that the probability of landing on red is $\frac{3}{8}$, on blue is $\frac{1}{4}$, on yellow is $\frac{1}{8}$, and on green is $\frac{1}{4}$.

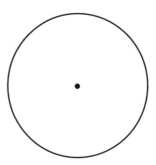

3. If you throw a 6-sided die 84 times, how many times would you expect a 4 to come up?

_____ times

Circle the word that best describes your chances of rolling a 4.

certain

likely

very unlikely

4. If you tossed a coin onto the grid below, what fraction of the tosses would you expect it to land on M?

_____ of the tosses

M	A	P
P	M	A
A	P	M

5. If you throw a 6-sided die 96 times, how many times would you expect it to land on a factor of 24?

_____ times

Explain. _____

_____

_____

_____

6. You flip a coin 9 times, and each time the coin lands on heads. If you flip the same coin one more time, is it more likely to come up heads than tails or just as likely to come up heads as tails? Explain.

_____

_____

_____

_____

_____

Statistics, Data Analysis, and Probability 2.0; Statistics, Data Analysis, and Probability 2.2

LESSON 9·8   Math Boxes

---

1. a. If you threw a 6-sided die 48 times, about how many times would you expect it to land on a number greater than or equal to 4?

_____ times

b. If you threw a 6-sided die 54 times, about how many times would you expect it to land on a number greater than 4?

_____ times

81

---

2. Name a percent value

a. greater than $\frac{1}{5}$ and less than $\frac{1}{2}$.

_____

b. less than $\frac{3}{4}$ and greater than $\frac{3}{5}$.

_____

61 62

---

3. Homer's is selling roller blades at 25% off the regular price of $52.00. Martin's is selling them for $\frac{1}{3}$ off the regular price of $60. Which store is offering the better buy?

_____

Show how you solved the problem.

38 39
59

---

4. If 1 centimeter on a map represents 300 kilometers, then 2.5 centimeters represents ____ kilometers. Choose the best answer.

 600

⬭ 650

⬭ 350

⬭ 750

145

---

5. What is the area of the triangle? Include the correct unit.

5"
11"

Number model: _____

Area = _____

136

---

6. a. Which is warmer, $-7°C$ or $-3.5°C$?

_____

How many degrees warmer?

_____

b. Which is colder, $-18°C$ or $-9.6°C$?

_____

How many degrees colder?

_____
60 139

LESSON 9·8 Multiplying Decimals

Math Message

Toni has 8 blocks. Each block is 1.2 centimeters high.
If she stacks the blocks, what will be the height of the stack?   _____ cm

1. Devon measured the length of the room by pacing it off.
   The length of his pace was 2.3 feet. He counted 14 paces.
   How long is the room?   _____ ft

2. Spiral notebooks are on sale for $0.35 each.
   How much will 25 spiral notebooks cost? $_____

3. Find the area of each rectangle below. Include the correct unit.
   Write a number model to show how you found the answer.

   a. 1.5 cm
      30 cm

      Number model: _____   Area = _____

   b. 6 in.
      15.4 in.

      Number model: _____   Area = _____

4. For each problem below, the multiplication has been done correctly, but the decimal point
   is missing in the answer. Write a number model to show how you estimated the answer.
   Then correctly place the decimal point in the answer.

   a. $23 * 7.3 =$ 1 6 7 9   b. $6.91 * 82 =$ 5 6 6 6 2

      Number model: Number model:

      _____   _____

   c. $5,203 * 12.6 =$ 6 5 5 5 7 8   d. $0.38 * 51 =$ 1 9 3 8

      Number model: Number model:

      _____   _____

Number Sense 3.3;Mathematical Reasoning 2.1

LESSON 9·8   Multiplying Decimals *continued*

Write a number model to estimate each product. Then multiply the factors as though they were whole numbers. Use your estimate to help you place the decimal in the answer.

5. 2.7 * 45 = _____

Number model: _____

6. 8 * 5.7 = _____

Number model: _____

7. 5.08 * 27 = _____

Number model: _____

8. 42 * 0.97 = _____

Number model: _____

Try This

9. 22 * 0.32 = _____

Number model:

_____

10. 0.02 * 333 = _____

Number model:

_____

LESSON 9·9   Dividing Decimals

1. Janine is building a bookshelf. She has a board that is 3.75 meters long. She wants to cut it into 5 pieces of equal length. What will be the length of each piece?

   _____ meters

2. Three sisters set up a lemonade stand. On Wednesday they made $8.46. If they shared the money equally, how much did each girl get?

   $_____

3. Alex and his three friends went out to lunch. The total bill, including tax and tip, was $42.52. They decided that each would pay the same amount. How much did each person pay?

   $_____

4. Victor divides a 98.4 cm piece of string into 3 equal pieces. What is the length of each piece?

   _____ centimeters

For each problem below, the division has been done correctly, but the decimal point is missing in the answer. Write a number model to show how to estimate the answer. Use your estimate to correctly place the decimal point in the answer.

5. $\dfrac{146}{3)43.8}$

   Number model: _____

6. $\dfrac{4982}{6)298.92}$

   Number model: _____

7. $\dfrac{1615}{4)6.46}$

   Number model: _____

8. $\dfrac{87}{5)4.35}$

   Number model: _____

Number Sense 3.4; Mathematical Reasoning 2.1

LESSON 9·9 Dividing Decimals *continued*

Write a number model to estimate each quotient. Then divide the numbers as though they were whole numbers. Use the estimate to help you place the decimal point in the answer.

9. _____ = 9.44 / 4

Number model: _____

10. 89.6 / 4 = _____

Number model: _____

11. 46.8 ÷ 12 = _____

Number model: _____

12. 253.8 / 6 = _____

Number model: _____

Try This

13. 2.96 / 8 = _____

Number model:

_____

14. _____ = 3.65 ÷ 5

Number model:

_____

LESSON 9·9 **Math Boxes**

---

1. Calculate.

   a. 10% of 90 = _____

   b. 5% of 140 = _____

   c. _____% of 30 = 24

   d. _____% of 48 = 36

   e. 20% of _____ = 9

---

2. Insert parentheses to make each number sentence true.

   a. 4 * 6 + 3 > 3 * 10

   b. 57 − 24 + 15 = 18

   c. 40 * 30 + 60 > 100 * 20

   d. 56 / 7 − 3 = 14

---

3. Complete the table with equivalent names.

Fraction	Decimal	Percent
		70%
	0.75	
3/5		
		72%

---

4. Divide. Use a paper-and-pencil algorithm.

268 ÷ 12 = _____

---

5. What is the area of the parallelogram? Include the correct unit.

Number model: _____

Area = _____

---

6. Study the figure. Draw the other half along the vertical line of symmetry.

---

1) AF 2.2   2) AF 1.3   3) NS 1.6
4) NS 3.2   5) MG 1.4   6) MG 3.4

LESSON
9·10

Math Boxes

---

1. Use a straightedge to draw the line of symmetry.

SRB
109

2. What temperature is it?

_____ °F

SRB
139

---

3. Draw the mirror image of the figure shown on the left of the vertical line.

SRB
106 109

4. a. Which is warmer, −9.4°C or −11.2°C?

_____

b. How many degrees warmer?

_____

c. Which is colder, −19.3°C or −12.8°C?

_____

d. How many degrees colder?

SRB
60 139

_____

---

5. Name four numbers greater than −8 and less than −5.

_____

_____

_____

_____

SRB
60

6. Name four numbers less than 2 and greater than −1.

_____

_____

_____

_____

SRB
60

LESSON 10·1   Basic Use of a Transparent Mirror

SRB 106

A **transparent mirror** is shown at the right.

Notice that the mirror has a **recessed** drawing edge, along which lines are drawn. Some transparent mirrors have a drawing edge both on the top and on the bottom.

Place your transparent mirror on this page so that its drawing edge lies along line *MK* below. Then look through the transparent mirror to read the "backward" message.

back face   end

front face

end   drawing edge

←————————————————————————————→

M   *K*

The following message is printed upside-down (to be read through the transparent mirror):

If you have followed the directions correctly, you are now able to read this message. Here are a few things to remember when using your transparent mirror:

◆ Always look into the front of the transparent mirror.
◆ In this position, the drawing edge will be facing you.
◆ Use your transparent mirror on flat surfaces like your desk or a tabletop.
◆ Use a sharp pencil when tracing along the drawing edge.
◆ Experiment and have fun!

Measurement and Geometry 3.4

LESSON 10·1 Math Boxes

1. Use your Geometry Template to draw the image of the figure that is shown on the right of the line of reflection.

image   preimage

 SRB 106

2. The following totals came up when Tina threw two dice:

4, 5, 9, 6, 12, 12, 2, 5, 6, 12, 3

a. What is the median? _____

b. Mode? _____

c. Maximum? _____

d. Minimum? _____

e. Range? _____

SRB 73

3. Order the fractions from least to greatest.

a. $\frac{8}{7}, \frac{5}{7}, \frac{3}{7}, \frac{1}{7}, \frac{4}{7}$ _____

b. $\frac{2}{4}, \frac{2}{3}, \frac{2}{5}, \frac{2}{9}, \frac{2}{12}$ _____

c. $\frac{3}{5}, \frac{9}{10}, \frac{4}{9}, \frac{1}{2}, \frac{2}{7}$ _____

SRB 53 54

4. Insert the decimal point in each product.

a. $8 * 9.6 = $ 7 6 8

b. 9 4 2 4 $= 19 * 4.96$

c. 7 4 2 $= 14 * 0.53$

d. $83 * 0.02 = $ 1 6 6

SRB 18 19

5. Miki took 40 shots in a basketball game. She missed 30% of the shots that she took.

a. What fraction of the shots did she miss?

_____

b. How many shots did she miss?

_____ shots

 SRB 38 39 62

6. What are the perimeter and area of the rectangle? Include the correct units.

3 ft

18 ft

Perimeter = _____

Area = _____

SRB 131 134

LESSON 10·2 **Finding Lines of Reflection**

Dart Game

Practice before you play the game on Activity Sheet 7. One partner chooses Dart A and the other partner Dart B. Try to hit the target with your own dart, using the transparent mirror. **Do not practice with your partner's dart.**

Now play the game with your partner.

Directions

Take turns. When it is your turn, use the other dart—the one you did not use for practice. Try to hit the target by placing the transparent mirror on the page, but **do not look through the mirror.** Then both you and your partner look through the mirror to see where the dart hit the target. Keep score.

Pocket-Billiards Game

Practice before you play the game on Activity Sheet 8. Choose a ball (1, 2, 3, or 4) and a pocket (A, B, C, D, E, or F). Try to get the ball into the pocket, using the transparent mirror.

Now play the game with a partner.

Directions

Take turns. When it is your turn, say which ball and which pocket you have picked: for example, "Ball 2 to go into Pocket D." Try to get the ball into the pocket by placing the transparent mirror on the billiard table, **but do not look through the mirror.** Then both you and your partner look through the mirror to check whether the ball has gone into the pocket.

1. How could measuring distances with a ruler help you place the mirror so that the ball goes into the pocket? For example, exactly where can you put the mirror so that Ball 2 will go into Pocket D?

   _____

   _____

   _____

Measurement and Geometry 3.4

Date _____ Time _____

LESSON 10·2 Math Boxes

---

1. Complete the table with equivalent names.

Fraction	Decimal	Percent
		29%
	0.30	
$\frac{8}{10}$		
		90%

61 62

---

2. Insert the decimal point in each quotient.

a. **2 8 2** = 84.6 ÷ 3

b. 91.6 ÷ 4 = **2 2 9**

c. **2 1 4** = 128.4 ÷ 6

d. 265.6 ÷ 8 = **3 3 2**

22 23

---

3. The fourth-grade students at Lighthouse School voted on their favorite season.

winter: 30 students

spring: 20 students

summer: 35 students

fall: 15 students

Use this data to create a bar graph.

76

---

4. Write the ordered pair for each point plotted on the coordinate grid.

A (___ , ___)

B (___ , ___)

C (___ , ___)

D (___ , ___)

E (___ , ___)

144

---

5. Write five names for −12.

a. _____

b. _____

c. _____

d. _____

e. _____

60

LESSON 10·3   Math Boxes

1. a. If you spin this spinner 400 times, about how many times would you expect it to land on

red? _____ times

blue? _____ times

b. Explain how you figured out how many times you would expect the spinner to land on blue.

_____

_____

_____

_____

SRB
82–86

---

2. Complete.

Rule: _____

in	out
$\frac{3}{8}$	$\frac{7}{8}$
$\frac{1}{6}$	
	$\frac{9}{10}$
$\frac{7}{20}$	
$\frac{1}{4}$	$\frac{3}{4}$

SRB
55 57

3. Solve each open sentence.

a. $32.5 + y = 37.6$ $y =$ _____

b. $123.5 - k = 102.2$ $k =$ _____

c. $b + 67.91 = 78.32$ $b =$ _____

d. $405.08 - w = 231.57$ $w =$ _____

SRB
34–37

---

4. Angle *ART* is an _____ (acute or obtuse) angle.

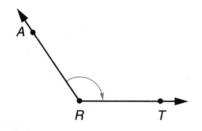

Measure of $\angle ART =$ _____ $^\circ$

SRB
93
142 143

5. Alberto and Lara estimated the weight of their adult cat. What is the most reasonable estimate? Fill in the circle next to the best answer.

○ **A.** 2 pounds

○ **B.** 10 pounds

○ **C.** 50 pounds

○ **D.** 100 pounds

SRB
140

---

1) SDAP 1.0   2. AF 1.4   3) AF 2.1
4) MG 3.5   5) MR 2.1

LESSON 10·4   Line Symmetry

You will need *Math Masters*, pages 311–314.

1. The drawings on *Math Masters*, page 311 are only half-pictures. Figure out what each whole picture would show. Then use a transparent mirror to complete each picture. Use the recessed side of the mirror to draw the line of reflection.

2. The pictures on *Math Masters*, page 312 are symmetric.

   a. Use the transparent mirror to draw the line of symmetry for the bat and the turtle.

   b. Cut out the other three pictures and find their lines of symmetry by folding.

   c. Which picture has two lines of symmetry? _____

3. Cut out each polygon on *Math Masters*, pages 313 and 314. Find all the lines of symmetry for each polygon. Record the results below.

Polygon	Number of Lines of Symmetry
A	3
B	1
C	4
D	2
E	2

Polygon	Number of Lines of Symmetry
F	0
G	1
H	0
I	5
J	6

4. Study the results in the tables above.

   a. How many lines of symmetry are in a regular pentagon (Polygon I)?   _____ lines

   b. How many lines of symmetry are in a regular hexagon (Polygon J)?   _____ lines

   c. How many lines of symmetry are in a regular octagon? (An octagon has 8 sides.)   _____ lines

LESSON 10·4 Math Boxes

1. Use your Geometry Template to draw the image of the figure that is shown above the line of reflection.

preimage

image

SRB
106

2. Use the following list of numbers to answer the questions.

7, 8, 24, 8, 9, 17, 17, 8, 12, 13, 19

a. What is the median? _____

b. Mode? _____

c. Maximum? _____

d. Minimum? _____

e. Range? _____

SRB
73

3. Order the fractions from least to greatest.

a. $\dfrac{8}{9}, \dfrac{4}{9}, \dfrac{1}{9}, \dfrac{9}{9}, \dfrac{3}{9}$ _____

b. $\dfrac{4}{4}, \dfrac{4}{9}, \dfrac{4}{12}, \dfrac{4}{3}, \dfrac{4}{2}$ _____

c. $\dfrac{3}{7}, \dfrac{1}{2}, \dfrac{7}{8}, \dfrac{1}{5}, \dfrac{4}{4}$ _____

SRB
53 54

4. Insert the decimal point in each product.

a. $4 * 6.7 =$ **2 6 8**

b. **1 4 5 6** $= 28 * 5.2$

c. $7.3 * 46 =$ **3 3 5 8**

d. **2 2 2 5** $= 0.25 * 89$

SRB
18 19

5. Jaleel missed 20% of the 30 problems on his science test. How many problems did he miss? Fill in the circle next to the best answer.

○ **A.** 5

○ **B.** 20

○ **C.** 3

○ **D.** 6

SRB
38
39 62

6. What are the perimeter and area of the rectangle? Include the correct units.

22 m

15 m

Perimeter = _____

Area = _____

SRB
131 134

1) MG 3.3   2) SDAP 1.2   3) NS 1.9
4) MR 2.2   5) AF 2.0   6) MG 1.4

Frieze Patterns

1. Extend the following frieze patterns. Use a straightedge and your transparent mirror to help you. Then write if you used a reflection, rotation, or translation of the original shape to continue the pattern.

a. _____

b. _____

c. _____

2. Create your own frieze pattern. Make a design in the first box. Then repeat the design, using reflections, slides, rotations, or a combination of moves. When you have finished, you may want to color or shade your frieze pattern.

3. Explain how you created your pattern in Problem 2.

_____

_____

LESSON 10·5 **Math Boxes**

1. Complete the table with equivalent names.

Fraction	Decimal	Percent
		31%
	0.10	
$\frac{4}{16}$		
		5%

61 62

2. Insert the decimal point in each quotient.

a. $74.8 \div 4 =$ **1 8 7**

b. **6 9** $= 34.5 \div 5$

c. $88.5 \div 3 =$ **2 9 5**

d. **2 4 2** $= 193.6 \div 8$

22 23

3. Julia babysat for the family next door. Below are the hours she worked.

Monday: 4 hours

Tuesday: $2\frac{1}{2}$ hours

Wednesday: 1 hour

Thursday: $1\frac{1}{2}$ hours

Friday: 3 hours

Use this data to create a bar graph.

___ ___ ___ ___ ___

_____

76

4. Write the ordered pair for each point plotted on the coordinate grid.

A (___ , ___)

B (___ , ___)

C (___ , ___)

D (___ , ___)

E (___ , ___)

144

5. Write five names for −73.

a. _____

b. _____

c. _____

d. _____

e. _____

60

1) NS 1.6   2) MR 2.2   3) SDAP 1.1
4) MG **2.0**   5) NS **1.8**

Review: Fractions, Decimals, and Percents

1. Fill in the missing numbers in the table of equivalent fractions, decimals, and percents.

Fraction	Decimal	Percent
$\frac{4}{10}$		
	0.6	
		75%

2. Kendra set a goal of saving $50 in 8 weeks. During the first 2 weeks, she was able to save $10.

   a. What fraction of the $50 did she save in the first 2 weeks? _____

   b. What percent of the $50 did she save? _____

   c. At this rate, how long will it take her to reach her goal? _____ weeks

3. Shade 80% of the square.

   a. What fraction of the square did you shade? _____

   b. Write this fraction as a decimal. _____

   c. What percent of the square is *not* shaded? _____

4. Tanara's new skirt was on sale at 15% off the original price. The original price of the skirt was $60.

   a. How much money did Tanara save with the discount? _____

   b. How much did she pay for the skirt? _____

5. Star Video and Vic's Video Mart sell videos at about the same regular prices. Both stores are having sales. Star Video is selling its videos at $\frac{1}{3}$ off the regular price. Vic's Video Mart is selling its videos at 25% off the regular price. Which store has the better sale? Explain your answer.

_____

_____

_____

LESSON 10·6   **Math Boxes**

1. a. Make a spinner. Color it so that if you spin it 36 times, you would expect it to land on blue 27 times and red 9 times.

b. Explain how you designed your spinner.

_____

_____

_____

_____

SRB
82–86

---

2. Complete.

Rule: _____

in	out
$\frac{8}{16}$	$\frac{4}{16}$
$\frac{8}{8}$	
$\frac{3}{4}$	$\frac{2}{4}$
	$\frac{7}{12}$
$\frac{15}{20}$	

SRB
55 57

---

3. Solve each open sentence.

a. $67.3 + p = 75.22$ $p =$ _____

b. $6.86 - a = 2.94$ $a =$ _____

c. $x + 5.69 = 7.91$ $x =$ _____

d. $4.6 - n = 0.32$ $n =$ _____

SRB
34–37

---

4. Angle *RUG* is an _____ (acute or obtuse) angle.

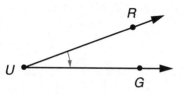

Measure of $\angle RUG =$ _____ °

SRB
93 142 143

---

5. Sebastian and Joshua estimated the weight of their mother. What is the most reasonable estimate? Fill in the circle next to the best answer.

○ **A.** 50 pounds

○ **B.** 150 pounds

○ **C.** 500 pounds

○ **D.** 1,000 pounds

SRB
140

---

1) SDAP 1.0   2) AF 1.4   3) AF 2.1
4) MG 3.5   5) MR 2.1

LESSON 10·7 Math Boxes

1. What is the area of the rectangle?

9 cm

4.8 cm

Area = _____ cm²

SRB
134

2. Write five names for −214.

a. _____

b. _____

c. _____

d. _____

e. _____

SRB
60

3. For each animal, circle the most reasonable estimate of its weight.

a. raccoon	> 500 pounds	< 500 pounds	about 500 pounds
b. tiger	> 500 pounds	< 500 pounds	about 500 pounds
c. blue whale	> 500 pounds	< 500 pounds	about 500 pounds
d. giraffe	> 500 pounds	< 500 pounds	about 500 pounds
e. squirrel	> 500 pounds	< 500 pounds	about 500 pounds

4. Draw 3 different rectangles. Each should have an area of 12 square centimeters. Next to each rectangle, record its perimeter.

SRB
131 134

LESSON 11·1 — Estimating Weights in Grams and Kilograms

A nickel weighs about 5 grams (5 g).
A liter of water weighs about 1 kilogram (1 kg).

In Problems 1–7, circle a possible weight for each object.

1. A dog might weigh about

   20 kg   200 kg   2,000 kg

2. A can of soup might weigh about

   4 g   40 g   400 g

3. A newborn baby might weigh about

   3 kg   30 kg   300 kg

4. An adult ostrich might weigh about

   1.5 kg   15 kg   150 kg

5. A basketball might weigh about

   0.6 kg   6 kg   60 kg

6. The weight limit in an elevator might be about

   100 kg   1,000 kg   10,000 kg

7. A pencil might weigh about

   4.5 g   45 g   450 g

8. Choose one of the problems above. Explain why you chose your answer.

   _____

   _____

Mathematical Reasoning 2.1

Date _____   Time _____

The number line below has ounces on the top and grams on the bottom.
It shows, for example, that 7 ounces are about equal to 200 grams.

ounces

grams

Use the number line to give the approximate weight of each object in grams.

1.   15 ounces

   About _____ grams

2.   16 ounces

   About _____ grams

3.   8 ounces

   About _____ grams

4.   2.3 ounces

   About _____ grams

Use the number line to give the approximate weight of each object in ounces.

5.   100 grams

   About _____ ounces

6.   500 grams

   About _____ ounces

7.   140 grams

   About _____ ounces

8.   454 grams

   About _____ ounces

LESSON 11·1 **Math Boxes**

---

1. a. Explain how you know that the pattern below is an example of a translation.

_____

_____

_____

b. Draw the figure after it is translated to the right.

SRB 107

---

2. Find the solution of each open sentence.

a. $\frac{6}{7} - y = \frac{4}{7}$ $y =$ _____

b. $\frac{3}{10} + a = \frac{9}{10}$ $a =$ _____

c. $\frac{3}{5} - r = \frac{1}{10}$ $r =$ _____

d. $\frac{3}{4} + m = \frac{7}{8}$ $m =$ _____

SRB 55 148

---

3. Circle the numbers that are multiples of 6. Put an X through the numbers that are multiples of 5.

38

84

150

198

540

3,500

SRB 9

---

4. Insert parentheses to make each number sentence true.

a. $14 * 18 - 15 = 42$

b. $13 - 6 * 5 = 56 - 21$

c. $48 / 6 + 2 = 10 - 4$

d. $150 / 10 + 5 < 4 * 4$

SRB 150

---

5. If you use an average of 7 sheets of paper per day, about how many sheets would you use in

a. 1 week? _____ sheets

b. 4 weeks? _____ sheets

c. 52 weeks? _____ sheets

d. 2 years? _____ sheets

SRB 47

---

1) MG 3.3   2) AF 2.1   3) NS 4.0
4) AF 1.3   5) NS 3.3

Geometric Solids

Geometric shapes like these 3-dimensional ones are also called **geometric solids.**

Rectangular   Cylinder   Triangular   Cone   Sphere   Square
Prism   Prism   Pyramid

Look around the classroom. Try to find examples of the geometric solids pictured
above. Draw a picture of each. Then write its name (for example: book).

Example of rectangular prism:	Example of cylinder:	Example of triangular prism:
Name of object:	Name of object:	Name of object:
_____	_____	_____
Example of cone:	Example of sphere:	Example of square pyramid:
Name of object:	Name of object:	Name of object:
_____	_____	_____

LESSON 11·2   Modeling a Rectangular Prism

After you construct a rectangular prism
with straws and twist-ties, answer
the questions below.

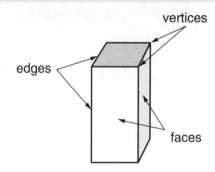

1. How many faces does your rectangular prism have? _____ face(s)

2. How many of these faces are formed by rectangles? _____ face(s)

3. How many of these faces are formed by squares? _____ face(s)

4. Pick one of the faces. How many other faces are parallel to it? _____ face(s)

5. How many edges does your rectangular prism have? _____ edge(s)

6. Pick an edge. How many other edges are parallel to it? _____ edge(s)

7. How many vertices does your rectangular prism have? _____ vertices

8. Write T (true) or F (false) for each of the following statements about the rectangular prism
   you made. Then write one true statement and one false statement of your own.

   a. _____ It has no curved surfaces.

   b. _____ All of the edges are parallel.

   c. _____ All of the faces are polygons.

   d. _____ All of the faces are congruent.

   e. True _____

   f. False _____

Measurement and Geometry 3.1; Measurement and Geometry 3.6

Making a 1-Ounce Weight

1. Estimate how many of each coin you think it will take to make a 1-ounce weight. Then use a balance or scale to determine exactly how many of each coin are needed.

Coin	Estimated Number of Coins	Actual Number of Coins
penny		
nickel		
dime		
quarter		

2. Describe how you estimated how many of each coin it might take to make a 1-ounce weight.

_____

_____

_____

_____

_____

_____

_____

Try This

3. About what fraction of an ounce does each coin weigh?

1 penny = _____ oz   1 nickel = _____ oz   1 dime = _____ oz   1 quarter = _____ oz

Explain how you found your answers.

_____

_____

_____

LESSON
11·2   **Math Boxes**

---

1. The object below has the shape of a geometric solid. What is the name of the solid? Circle the best answer.

A. rectangular prism

B. cone

C. cylinder

D. square pyramid

101 102

---

2. Draw the figure after it is rotated clockwise $\frac{1}{4}$-turn.

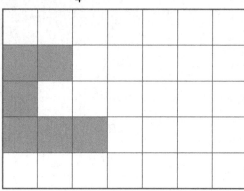

SRB
106 107

---

3. Write a number model to estimate the answer. Then correctly place the decimal point.

a. $0.97 * 4 = 3\ 8\ 8$

Number model: _____

b. $1\ 8\ 7 = 74.8 \div 4$

Number model: _____

---

4. Insert $<$, $>$, or $=$ to make a true number sentence.

a. -12 _____ -19

b. -44 _____ 26

c. -64 _____ -0.43

d. $-\frac{1}{2}$ _____ $-\frac{4}{8}$

e. -0.28 _____ -0.37

SRB
6   60

---

5. Round each number to the nearest tenth.

a. 2.34 _____

b. 0.68 _____

c. 14.35 _____

d. 1.62 _____

e. 5.99 _____

SRB
182 183

---

6. A cinnamon raisin bagel has about 230 calories. How many calories are in one dozen bagels?

About _____ calories

47

---

1) MG 3.6   2) MG 3.4   3) MR 2.1
4) AF 1.0   5) NS 2.2   6) NS 3.3

LESSON 11·3   Construction of Polyhedrons

Polyhedrons are geometric solids with flat surfaces formed by polygons.

For each problem below—

◆ Decide what the polyhedron should look like.

◆ Use straws and twist-ties to model the polyhedron.

◆ Answer the questions about the polyhedron.

Look at page 102 of the *Student Reference Book*
if you need help with the name.

1. I am a polyhedron.
    I have 5 faces.
    Four of my faces are formed by triangles.
    One of my faces is a square.

    a. After you make me, draw a picture of me in the
       space to the right.

    b. What am I?   _____

    c. How many corners (vertices) do I have?   _____

    d. What shape is my base?   _____

2. I am a polyhedron.
    I have 4 faces.
    All of my faces are formed by equilateral triangles.
    All of my faces are the same size.

    a. After you make me, draw a picture of me in the
       space to the right.

    b. What am I?   _____

    c. How many corners (vertices) do I have?   _____

    d. What shape is my base?   _____

LESSON 11·3 Drawing a Cube

Knowing how to draw is a useful skill in mathematics. Here are a few ways to draw a cube. Try each way. Tape your best work at the bottom of page 295.

A Basic Cube

Draw a square.

Draw another square that overlaps your first square.
The second square should be the same size as the first.

Connect the corners of your 2 squares as shown.
This picture does not look much like a real cube. One problem is that the picture shows all 12 edges, even though not all the edges of a real cube can be seen at one time. Another problem is that it is hard to tell which face of the cube is in front.

A Better Cube

Begin with a square.

Next, draw 3 parallel line segments going right and up from 3 corners of your square. The segments should all be the same length.

Finally, connect the ends of the 3 line segments.

This cube is better than before, but it shows only the edges and corners, not the faces. If you want, try shading your cube to make it look more realistic.

Measurement and Geometry 3.0; Measurement and Geometry 3.6

LESSON 11·3 Drawing a Cube *continued*

A Cube with Hidden Edges

Sometimes people draw cubes and other shapes with dashed line segments.
The dashed line segments show edges that are hidden. Here is one way to draw
a cube with hidden edges. Use a pencil.

Draw a square.

Draw a faint square that overlaps your first square.
The second square should be the same size as the first.

Connect the corners of your 2 squares with faint line segments.

Trace over 5 of your faint line segments with solid lines
and 3 with dashed lines. The dashed line segments show the
3 edges that are hidden.

Tape your best work here.

LESSON
11·3 **Math Boxes**

---

1. Draw the figure after it is translated to the right.

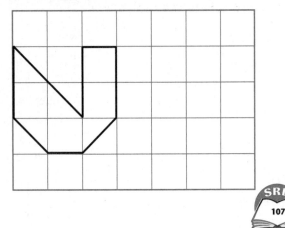

SRB
107

---

2. Find the solution of each open sentence.

a. $\frac{7}{8} - s = \frac{1}{8}$ $s =$ _____

b. $t + \frac{1}{4} = \frac{1}{2}$ $t =$ _____

c. $\frac{3}{10} - m = \frac{1}{5}$ $m =$ _____

d. $\frac{2}{8} + x = \frac{3}{4}$ $x =$ _____

SRB
55   148

---

3. Name the first ten multiples of each number.

a. 6 _____, _____, _____, _____, _____, _____, _____, _____, _____, _____

b. 86 _____, _____, _____, _____, _____, _____, _____, _____, _____, _____

SRB
9

---

4. Insert parentheses to make each number sentence true.

a. $98.3 + 1.7 * 2.5 = 250$

b. $21.7 / 3 + 4 = 3.1$

c. $56.3 + 3.7 * 3 > 5 * 30$

d. $13.8 - 8.3 = 26.15 - 23.4 * 2$

SRB
150

---

5. Gum costs $0.80 per pack. What is the cost of

a. 4 packs of gum? _____

b. 10 packs of gum? _____

c. 16 packs of gum? _____

d. 33 packs of gum? _____

---

1) MG 3.3   2) AF 2.1   3) NS 4.0
4) AF 1.3   5) NS 3.3

LESSON 11·4 Math Boxes

1. The object below has the shape of a geometric solid. Name the solid.

_____

SRB 101

2. Draw the figure after it is rotated counterclockwise $\frac{1}{4}$-turn.

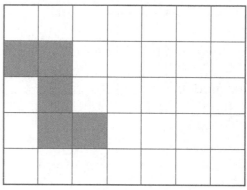

SRB 106 107

3. Write a number model to estimate the answer. Then correctly place the decimal point.

a. $7.56 * 4 = 3\ 0\ 2\ 4$

Number model: _____

b. $563.2 \div 4 = 1\ 4\ 0\ 8$

Number model: _____

4. Insert $<$, $>$, or $=$ to make a true number sentence.

a. -14 _____ -6

b. -123 _____ -241

c. -8.9 _____ -5.7

d. $-\frac{1}{4}$ _____ $-\frac{2}{5}$

e. $-\frac{3}{9}$ _____ $-\frac{1}{3}$

SRB 6 60

5. Round each number to the nearest tenth.

a. 3.46 _____

b. 0.71 _____

c. 4.35 _____

d. 9.60 _____

e. 22.89 _____

SRB 182 183

6. Jake can ride his bike 5 miles in 40 minutes. At this rate, how long does it take him to ride 1 mile? Circle the best answer.

A. 200 minutes

B. 40 minutes

C. 20 minutes

D. 8 minutes

Date _____ Time _____

1. Write a formula for the area of a rectangle. In your formula, use *A* for area. Use *l* and *w* for length and width, or *b* and *h* for base and height.

   _____

2. Draw a rectangle with sides measuring 3 centimeters and 9 centimeters. Find the area.

   Number model: _____   Area = _____ square centimeters

3. Find the height of the rectangle.

   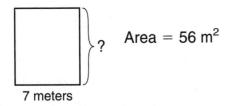

   Number model: _____

   height = _____ m

4. Find the length of the base of the rectangle.

   Number model: _____

   length of base = _____ in.

Try This

5. Find the area of the rectangle.

   Number model: _____

   Area = _____ cm²

6. Find the height of the rectangle.

   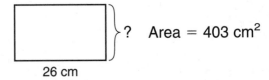

   Number model: _____

   height = _____ cm

Measurement and Geometry 1.4; Algebra and Functions 1.1; Algebra and Functions 1.4

LESSON 11·5   **Math Boxes**

---

1. What is the total number of cubes needed to completely fill the box?

_____ cubes

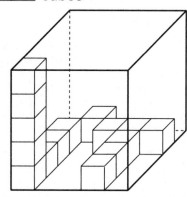

SRB
138

2. Calculate the volume.

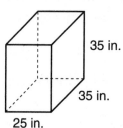

35 in.

35 in.

25 in.

Number model: _____

Volume = _____ in³

SRB
138

---

3. When you roll a 6-sided die, about what fraction of the time would you expect

a. a multiple of 2 to come up?   _____

b. a factor of 20 to come up?   _____

SRB
81

4. Complete.

a. 13 ft = _____ yd _____ ft

b. 18 ft 6 in. = _____ yd _____ in.

c. 972 in. = _____ yd

d. 15,840 ft = _____ mi

e. 24,640 yd = _____ mi

SRB
129

---

5. Add.

a. $-54 + 28 =$ _____

b. $-62 + (-15) =$ _____

c. _____ $= 51 + (-139)$

d. _____ $= -\$23.56 + \$87.45$

e. $\$71.08 + (-\$85.79) =$ _____

6. If 4 shirts cost $76, what is the cost of

a. 2 shirts? _____

b. 6 shirts? _____

c. 1 dozen shirts? _____

d. 75 shirts? _____

SRB
47

LESSON 11·5 Cube-Stacking Problems

Each picture at the bottom of this page and on the next page shows a box that is partially filled with cubes. The cubes in each box are the same size. Each box has at least one stack of cubes that goes to the top.

Your task is to find the total number of cubes needed to completely fill each box.

Record your answers in the table below.

Table of Volumes						
Placement of Cubes	**Box 1**	**Box 2**	**Box 3**	**Box 4**	**Box 5**	**Box 6**
Number of cubes needed to cover the bottom						
Number of cubes in the tallest stack (Be sure to count the bottom cube.)						
Total number of cubes needed to fill the box						

Box 1

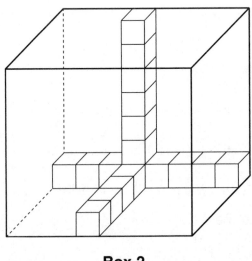

Box 2

Algebra and Functions 1.1

Cube-Stacking Problems *continued*

Box 3

Box 4

Box 5

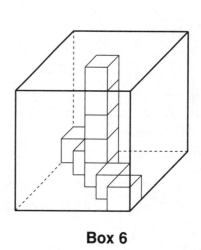

Box 6

Formula for the volume of a rectangular prism:

_____

B is the **area** of a base.

h is the height from that base.

Volume units are cubic units.

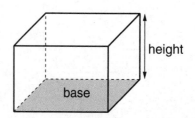

height

base

LESSON 11·5 **Cube-Stacking Problems** *continued*

Find the volume of each stack of centimeter cubes.

1.

Volume = _____ cm³

2.

Volume = _____ cm³

3.

Volume = _____ cm³

4.

Volume = _____ cm³

5. Choose one of the problems from above. Describe the strategy that you used to find the volume of the stack of centimeter cubes.

_____

_____

_____

Try This

6.

3 cm

3 cm

2 cm

Number model: _____

Volume = _____ cm³

7.

2 cm

10 cm

8 cm

Number model: _____

Volume = _____ cm³

Algebra and Functions 1.1; Algebra and Functions 1.4; Mathematical Reasoning 2.2

LESSON 11·6 Gram and Ounce Museum

1. **a.** What was the heaviest item in the class Gram and Ounce Museum? _____

    b. How much did it weigh? _____ grams   _____ ounces

2. **a.** What was the lightest item in the class Gram and Ounce Museum? _____

    b. How much did it weigh? _____ grams   _____ ounces

Complete.

3. 6 g = _____ mg

4. _____ g = 7,000 mg

5. 3 kg = _____ g

6. _____ kg = 8,000 g

7. 2.9 g = _____ mg

8. _____ kg = 4,500 g

9. 6 lb = _____ oz

10. _____ lb = 144 oz

11. 3.5 lb = _____ oz

12. 8 T = _____ lb

Use the Rules of Thumb below to solve Problems 13–15. Write number models to show how you estimated.

> **Rules of Thumb**
>
> 1 kilogram equals about 2.2 pounds
> 1 ounce equals about 30 grams

13. A video camera weighs about 120 grams. About how many ounces is that?

    Number model: _____   _____ oz

14. A baby weighs about 3.5 kilograms at birth. About how many pounds is that?

    Number model: _____   _____ lb

15. An African elephant weighs 11,023 pounds. About how many kilograms is that?

    Number model: _____   _____ kg

LESSON 11·6 Math Boxes

1. The object below has the shape of a geometric solid. Name the solid.

_____

101

2. Which figure below shows the original figure rotated clockwise $\frac{1}{2}$-turn?

_____

Original   A   B   C

SRB
106 107

3. Write a number model to estimate the answer. Then correctly place the decimal point.

a. $6 * 32.9 = 1\ 9\ 7\ 4$

Number model: _____

b. $3\ 2\ 9 = 98.7 \div 3$

Number model: _____

4. Insert $<$, $>$, or $=$ to make a true number sentence.

a. -34 _____ -9

b. -89 _____ -99

c. -2.99 _____ -2.9

d. $-\frac{1}{4}$ _____ $-\frac{1}{3}$

e. $-\frac{18}{9}$ _____ $-2\frac{1}{4}$

6   60

5. Round 8.99 to the nearest tenth. Circle the best answer.

A. 8.0

B. 9.0

C. 9.1

D. 8.09

182 183

6. It takes 2 cups of flour to make about 20 medium-size peanut butter cookies. How many cups of flour will you need to make about

a. 40 cookies? _____ cups

b. 60 cookies? _____ cups

c. 50 cookies? _____ cups

d. 740 cookies? _____ cups

47

1) MG 3.6   2) MG 3.4   3) MR 2.1
4) AF 1.0   5) NS 2.2   6) NS 3.3

LESSON 11·7 Converting Measurements

Math Message

1 pint = _____ cups

1 quart = _____ pints

1 half-gallon = _____ quarts

1 gallon = _____ quarts

Think: How can the picture above help you remember how many cups are in a pint, how many pints are in a quart, and how many quarts are in a gallon?

Rice Consumption

1. Round your answer to the nearest ounce.

   One cup of dry (uncooked) rice weighs about _____ ounces.

2. Use the answer in Problem 1 to complete the following:

   a. 1 pint of rice weighs about _____ ounces.

   b. 1 quart of rice weighs about _____ ounces.

   c. 1 gallon of rice weighs about _____ ounces.

   d. 1 gallon of rice weighs about _____ pounds. (1 pound = 16 ounces)

3. On average, a family of 4 in Bangladesh eats about 170 pounds of rice per month.

   a. That is about how many pounds per year? _____ pounds

   b. How many gallons? _____ gallons

4. On average, a family of 4 in the United States eats about 120 pounds of rice per year. That is about how many gallons per year? _____ gallons

5. On average, a family of 4 in Thailand eats about $3\frac{1}{2}$ gallons of rice per week.

   a. That is about how many gallons per year? _____ gallons

   b. How many pounds? _____ pounds

LESSON 11·7 Largest Cities by Population

1. Use the data in the Largest Cities by Population table at the top of *Student Reference Book*, page 302 to complete the bar graph. Round each figure to the nearest million.

Largest Cities by Population

Number of People (in millions)

36 34 32 30 28 26 24 22 20 18 16 14 12 10

Tokyo   Mexico City   New York City   São Paulo   Mumbai (Bombay)   Calcutta   Shanghai

Cities

2. Make three statements comparing the cities in the bar graph.

Example: *About 21 million more people live in Tokyo than in Shanghai.*

_____

_____

_____

_____

_____

Statistics, Data Analysis, and Probability 1.0

LESSON 11·7   Math Boxes

1. What is the total number of cubes needed to completely fill the box?

_____ cubes

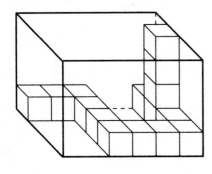

SRB 138

2. Calculate the volume.

2 cm
5 cm
9 cm

Number model: _____

Volume = _____ cm³

 SRB 138

3. When you roll a 10-sided die, about what fraction of the time would you expect a multiple of 3 to come up?

_____

Use a probability term to describe the likelihood of this event.

_____

SRB 81

4. Complete.

a. 321 cm = _____ m

b. 56 cm = _____ mm

c. 14 ft 4 in. = _____ in.

d. 2 mi = _____ ft

e. 5.3 km = _____ m

f. _____ mi = 7,040 yd

 SRB 129

5. Add.

a. $-46 + 20 =$ _____

b. $-23 + (-18) =$ _____

c. _____ $= 33 + (-17)$

d. _____ $= \$36.54 + (-\$57.81)$

e. $-\$131.09 + (-\$76.98) =$ _____

6. If you travel at an average speed of 50 miles per hour, how far will you travel in

a. 3 hours? _____ miles

b. $\frac{1}{2}$ hour? _____ miles

c. $2\frac{1}{2}$ hours? _____ miles

d. $5\frac{3}{5}$ hours? _____ miles

 SRB 47

LESSON 11·8 Math Boxes

1. If you use the telephone an average of 4 times per day, about how many times would you use it in

a. 1 week? __28__ times

b. 4 weeks? __56__ times

c. 52 weeks? __112__ times

SRB 47

2. A cup of orange juice has about 110 calories. About how many calories are in a quart of orange juice?

__440__ calories

SRB 47

3. Pears cost $0.55 each. What is the cost of

a. 4 pears? __$220__

b. 10 pears? __$5.52__

c. 18 pears? __$4.95__

SRB 47

4. If you walk at an average speed of 3.5 miles per hour, how far will you travel in

a. 2 hours? _____ miles

b. 6 hours? _____ miles

c. $\frac{1}{2}$ hour? _____ miles

SRB 47

5. Michelle can run 5 miles in 35 minutes. At this rate, how long does it take her to run 1 mile?

_____ minutes

SRB 47

6. Round each number to the nearest tenth.

a. 5.87 _____

b. 0.32 _____

c. 9.65 _____

d. 3.40 _____

e. 93.29 _____

SRB 182 183

1) NS 3.3   2) NS 3.3   3) NS 3.3
4) MR 2.2   5) NS 3.4   6) NS 2.2

LESSON 12·1   **Rates**

1. While at rest, a typical student in my class blinks _____ times in one minute.

2. While reading, a typical student in my class blinks _____ times in one minute.

3. In Problems 1 and 2, what is meant by the phrase *a typical student?*

   _____

   _____

4. Calculate the mean for each set of data.

   a. At rest: _____ blinks per minute

   b. While reading: _____ blinks per minute

5. List as many examples of rates as you can.

   _____

   _____

   _____

   _____

6. Find at least 2 examples of rates in your *Student Reference Book.*
   (*Hint:* Look at pages 271 and 299.)

   _____

   _____

   _____

   _____

LESSON 12·1 Counting with Fractions and Decimals

Fill in the missing fractions on the number lines below.

1.

2.

3.

Fill in the missing decimals on the number lines below.

4.

Try This

5.

6.

Number Sense 1.9

LESSON 12·1 Math Boxes

1.

a. Pick a face of the cube. How many other faces are parallel to it?

_____ face(s)

b. Pick an edge of the cube. How many other edges are parallel to it?

_____ edge(s)

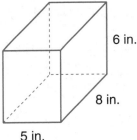

2. Calculate the volume.

6 in.

8 in.

5 in.

Number model: _____

Volume = _____ in³

3. Write A, P, or V to tell whether you would need to find the area, perimeter, or volume in each situation.

a. Finding the distance around a circular track _____

b. Buying tile for a bathroom floor _____

c. Filling a pool with water _____

4. Insert <, >, or = to make a true number sentence.

a. −15 _____ 3

b. −43 _____ −21

c. 68 _____ −100

d. −$\frac{3}{4}$ _____ −0.78

e. −13$\frac{1}{2}$ _____ −13

5. For which number is 8 a factor? Fill in the circle next to the best answer.

Ⓐ 253

Ⓑ 94

Ⓒ 120

Ⓓ 884

6. Round each number to the nearest hundredth.

a. 12.368 _____

b. 234.989 _____

c. 1.225 _____

d. 12.304 _____

e. 0.550 _____

LESSON 12·2 Rate Tables

For each problem, fill in the rate table. Then answer the question below the table.

1. Bill's new car can travel about 35 miles on 1 gallon of gasoline.

Gasoline mileage: 35 miles per gallon

Miles	35							
Gallons	1	2	3	4	5	6	7	8

At this rate, about how far can the car travel on 7 gallons of gas? _____ miles

2. Jennifer earns $8 for every 4 hours she helps out around the house.

Earnings: $8 in 4 hours

Dollars				8				
Hours	1	2	3	4	5	6	7	8

At this rate, how much money does Jennifer earn per hour? $_____

3. A gray whale's heart beats 24 times in 3 minutes.

Gray whale's heart rate: 24 beats in 3 minutes

Heartbeats			24					
Minutes	1	2	3	4	5	6	7	8

At this rate, how many times does a gray whale's heart beat in 2 minutes? _____ times

4. Ms. Romero paid $1.80 for 3 pounds of grapes.

Cost of grapes: 3 pounds for $1.80

Pounds	1	2	3	4	5	6	7	8
Dollars			1.80					

At this rate, how much do 5 pounds of grapes cost? $_____

Mathematical Reasoning 3.3; Number Sense 3.0

LESSON 12·2   Rate Tables *continued*

5. Malia bought 6 yards of fabric for $15.00.

Cost of fabric: 6 yards for $15.00

Dollars						15.00		
Yards	1	2	3	4	5	6	7	8

At this rate, how much will $7\frac{1}{2}$ yards of fabric cost? $ _____

6. Alden bought $\frac{3}{4}$ of a pound of cheese for $6.

Cost of cheese: $\frac{3}{4}$ of a pound for $6

Pounds	$\frac{1}{4}$	$\frac{1}{2}$	$\frac{3}{4}$	1	$1\frac{1}{4}$	$1\frac{1}{2}$	$1\frac{3}{4}$	2
Dollars			6					

At this rate, how much will $1\frac{1}{4}$ pounds cost? $ _____

Try This

7. The Jefferson family plans to sit down to Thanksgiving dinner at 6:00 P.M. They have an 18-pound turkey. The turkey needs to cook about 20 minutes per pound.

   a. At what time should the turkey go in the oven? _____

   b. Explain what you did to solve the problem.

   _____

   _____

   _____

   _____

LESSON 12·2

Math Boxes

1. a. Complete the table.

Number of Pizzas	1	2		4	5
Number of Servings	3		9	12	

b. How many pizzas are needed for 279 servings?

_____ pizzas

47

2. Complete.

a. 3 gal = _____ qt

b. 4 qt = _____ pt

c. 6 pt = _____ c

d. _____ pt _____ c = 23 c

e. 64 gal = _____ pt

137

3. Find the solution of each open sentence.

a. $m + 40 = -60$ $m =$ _____

b. $55 + q = 40$ $q =$ _____

c. $(-23) + s = 0$ $s =$ _____

d. $p + (-36) = -80$ $p =$ _____

148

4. Complete the name-collection box.

8.01

149

5. Fill in the blank with one of the words below.

impossible

unlikely

likely

Without looking, it is _____ that a B block will be pulled from the bag.

80

6. Calculate.

a. 10% of 460 = _____

b. 5% of 120 = _____

c. 40% of _____ = 4

d. _____% of 20 = 6

e. _____% of 92 = 46

f. _____% of 150 = 57

38 39

1) MR 3.2   2) MR 1.1   3) AF 1.2
4) AF 2.0   5) SDAP 2.0   6) AF 2.2

LESSON 12·3

Math Boxes

1.

   a. Pick a face of the cube. How many other faces are perpendicular to it?

   _____ face(s)

   b. Pick an edge of the cube. How many other edges are perpendicular to it? _____ edge(s)

SRB 94 101

2. Calculate the volume.

9 m
5 m
1 m

Number model: _____

Volume = _____ m³

SRB 138

3. Write A, P, or V to tell whether you would need to find the area, perimeter, or volume in each situation.

   a. Buying paint for a bedroom ceiling _____

   b. Buying a wedding ring _____

   c. Buying dirt for a potted plant _____

SRB 131 133 137

4. Insert <, >, or = to make a true number sentence.

   a. $8 _____ −$3

   b. −$7 _____ −$2

   c. $18 _____ −$11

   d. $61.50 _____ −$67.85

   e. −$203.90 _____ $320.10

SRB 60

5. Name all the factors of each number.

   a. 55 _____

   b. 32 _____

   c. 96 _____

SRB 7

6. Round each number to the nearest hundredth.

   a. 0.123 _____

   b. 4.568 _____

   c. 6.155 _____

   d. 9.780 _____

   e. 0.006 _____

SRB 182 183

Math Message

It is estimated that the average lifetime of a person living in the United States is about 75 years.

About how many days are there in an average lifetime? _____ days

About how many hours is that? _____ hours

Use the data from the above Math Message to help you answer the following questions:

1. It is estimated that a person sleeps about 214,000 hours in an average lifetime.

   a. At that rate, about how many hours *per day* does a person sleep? _____ hours per day

   b. Show or explain how you got your answer.

   c. Does this number make sense to you? Explain.

   _____

   _____

2. It is estimated that in an average lifetime a person watches about 105,000 hours of TV.

   a. At that rate, about how many hours *per day* does a person watch TV? _____ hours per day

   b. Show or explain how you got your answer.

   c. Does this number make sense to you? Explain.

   _____

   _____

Number Sense 2.2, **3.3**, **3.4**; Mathematical Reasoning 3.1

LESSON 12·3 Do These Numbers Make Sense? *continued*

3. It is estimated that in an average lifetime a person laughs about 540,000 times.

   a. At that rate, about how many times *per day* does a person laugh? _____ times per day

   b. Show or explain how you got your answer.

   c. Does this number make sense to you? Explain.

   _____

   _____

   _____

4. It is estimated that in an average lifetime, a person takes about 95,000,000 breaths. Does this number make sense to you? Explain.

   _____

   _____

   _____

Try This

5. Write your own problem. Ask a partner to decide whether or not the numbers in your problem make sense.

   _____

   _____

   _____

Number Sense 2.2, 3.3 , 3.4 ; Mathematical Reasoning 3.1

SRB 79

LESSON 12·3 Line Graph

1. Use the data in the table below to create a line graph showing how the total amount of precipitation (rain and snow) changes from month to month in Ottawa, the capital of Canada.

Use a straightedge to connect the points. Label each axis, and give the graph a title.

Month	J	F	M	A	M	J	J	A	S	O	N	D
Precipitation (in mm)	51	50	57	65	77	84	87	88	84	75	81	73

Source: www.theweathernetwork.com/weather/stats/pages/C01930.htm

---

Try This

2. In Ottawa, Canada, it rains or snows _____ mm during a typical month.

Measurement and Geometry **2.0**; Statistics, Data Analysis, and Probability 1.0

LESSON 12·4 Product Testing

Some publications written for young people ask their readers to test many different kinds of products. The results of the tests are then published to help readers make wise buying decisions. An excellent example is the Web site *Consumer Reports for Kids Online* at www.zillions.org. It features articles previously published in *Zillions,* a child's version of *Consumer Reports*. In one test, 99 readers field-tested several backpack models. The readers considered fit, back friendliness, and comfort as they tried to decide which brand was the best buy. In another test, a team of young people compared 40 brands of jeans in their search for a brand that would not shrink in length.

When a reader wrote to complain about a board game she bought, the staff sent board games to young people in every part of the country. Testers were asked to play each game several times and then to report what they liked and disliked about the game.

1. If you were testing a board game, what are some of the features you would look for?

_____

_____

_____

_____

2. When readers of the magazine tested backpacks, they considered fit, back friendliness, and comfort in determining the best one. Which of these factors is the most important to you? Why?

_____

_____

_____

3. What is a **consumer**? Be prepared to share your definition with the class.

_____

_____

_____

_____

LESSON 12·4 Unit Prices

Solve the unit price problems below. Complete the tables if it is helpful to do so.

1. A 12-ounce can of fruit juice costs 60 cents. The unit price is _____ per ounce.

Dollars				0.60
Ounces	1	3	6	12

2. A 4-pound bunch of bananas costs $1.16. The unit price is _____ per pound.

Dollars				1.16
Pounds	1	2	3	4

3. A 5-pound bag of apples costs $1.90. The unit price is _____ per pound.

Dollars					1.90
Pounds	1	2	3	4	5

4. Three pounds of salmon cost $21.00.

   a. The unit price is _____ per pound.

   b. What is the cost of 7 pounds of salmon? _____

   c. What is the cost of $9\frac{1}{2}$ pounds of salmon? _____

Dollars			21.00			
Pounds	1	2	3	4	7	$9\frac{1}{2}$

Try This

5. *Energy* granola bars come in packages of 25 and cost $3.50 per package. *Super* granola bars come in packages of 30 and cost $3.60 per package. Which is the better buy? Explain.

_____

_____

_____

Number Sense 3.3; Number Sense 3.4

Math Boxes

1. a. Complete the table.

Number of Inches		72			540
Number of Yards	1	2	9	12	

b. How many inches are in 329 yards?

_____ inches

SRB
47

2. Complete.

a. 7 gal = _____ qt

b. 3 qt = _____ pt

c. 8 pt = _____ c

d. _____ gal _____ qt = 25 qt

e. _____ qt _____ pt = 14 c

SRB
137

3. Find the solution of each open sentence.

a. $t + 30 = -120$ $t =$ _____

b. $75 + n = 20$ $n =$ _____

c. $16 + b = 0$ $b =$ _____

d. $c + (-61) = -97$ $c =$ _____

SRB
148

4. Which one of the names below is *not* a name for 3.16? Fill in the circle next to the best answer.

Ⓐ $4.8 - 1.64$

Ⓑ $15.8 / 5$

Ⓒ $2.47 * 6$

Ⓓ $2.5 + 0.66$

SRB
149

5. Add blocks to the bag so it is likely that Arjan will pick a C block without looking.

SRB
80

6. Calculate.

a. 10% of 520 = _____

b. 5% of 180 = _____

c. 40% of _____ = 4

d. _____% of 30 = 15

e. _____% of 35 = 14

f. _____% of 95 = 38

SRB
38 39

LESSON 12·5 Unit Pricing

Math Message

1. Use your calculator to divide. Write down what the calculator displays for each quotient. Your teacher will tell you how to fill in the answer spaces for "cents."

   a. $9.52 ÷ 7 = $_____._____, or _____ cents

   b. $1.38 ÷ 6 = $_____._____, or _____ cents

   c. $0.92 ÷ 8 = $_____._____, or _____ cents

   d. $0.98 ÷ 6 = $_____._____, or about _____ cents

   e. $1.61 ÷ 9 = $_____._____, or about _____ cents

2. A package of 6 fruit bars costs $2.89. What is the price of 1 fruit bar?   _____ cents

3. A 15-ounce bottle of shampoo costs $3.89. What is the price per ounce? _____ cents

4. Brand A: a box of 16 crayons for 80 cents
   Brand B: a box of 32 crayons of the same kind for $1.28

   Which box is the better buy?   _____

   Why? _____

   _____

   _____

   _____

   Try This

5. A store sells a 3-pound can of coffee for $7.98 and a 2-pound can of the same brand for $5.98. You can use a coupon worth 70 cents toward the purchase of the 2-pound can. If you use the coupon, which is the better buy, the 3-pound can or the 2-pound can? Explain your answer.

   _____

   _____

   _____

   _____

Number Sense **3.4**

LESSON 12·5 **Math Boxes**

---

1. Multiply. Show your work.

$46 * 231 =$ _____

 18 19

---

2. a. Complete the table.

Number of Cups		32			272
Number of Gallons	1	2	9	12	

b. How many cups are in $5\frac{3}{4}$ gallons?

_____ cups

47

---

3. An average 10-year-old drinks about 20 *gallons* of soft drinks per year.

At that rate, about how many *cups* does a 10-year-old drink in a month?

_____

47

---

4. Subtract.

a. $+\$9 - (+\$4) =$ _____

b. $+\$8 - (-\$3) =$ _____

c. $-\$7 - (+\$15) =$ _____

d. $-\$6 - (+\$1) =$ _____

e. $-\$14 - (-\$9) =$ _____

 60

---

5. Calculate the volume.

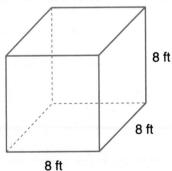

8 ft

8 ft

8 ft

Number model: _____

Volume = _____ ft³

138

---

6. A 3-ounce bag of corn chips costs $0.65. A 14-ounce bag of corn chips costs $2.79.

a. What is the price per ounce of each bag? (Round to the nearest cent.)

3-oz bag: _____

14-oz bag: _____

b. Which bag of chips is the better buy?

_____

 47

Looking Back on the World Tour

Math Message

It is time to complete the World Tour.

1. Fly to Washington, D.C., and then travel to your hometown. Mark the final leg of the tour on the Route Map on *Math Journal 2,* pages 330 and 331.

2. What is the total distance you have traveled? _____ miles

3. The airline has given you a coupon for every 5,000 miles you have traveled. Suppose you did all your traveling by plane on the same airline. How many coupons have you earned on the World Tour? _____ coupons

4. You can trade in 5 coupons for one free round-trip ticket to fly anywhere in the continental United States. How many round-trip tickets have you earned on the World Tour? _____ round-trip tickets

Refer to "My Country Notes" in your journals (*Math Journal 1,* pages 174–181 and *Math Journal 2,* pages 332–341) as you answer the following questions.

5. If you could travel all over the world for a whole year, what information would you need in order to plan your trip?

_____

_____

_____

_____

_____

_____

_____

_____

_____

Number Sense **3.0**; Mathematical Reasoning 2.3

LESSON 12·6   **Looking Back on the World Tour** *continued*

6. To which country would you most like to travel in your lifetime? Explain your answer.

_____

_____

_____

_____

_____

7. On your travels, you would have the opportunity to learn about many different cultures. What would you want to share with people from other countries about *your* culture?

_____

_____

_____

_____

_____

8. What are some things you have enjoyed on the World Tour?

_____

_____

_____

_____

_____

9. What is something about the World Tour you would like to add or change?

_____

_____

_____

_____

_____

LESSON 12·6 Rates

1. David Fischer of Chicago, Illinois, jumped rope 56 times in 60 seconds. If he could continue at this rate, about how many jumps would he do in 13 minutes?

   About _____ jumps

   Source: Guinness World Records, www.guinnessworldrecords.com

2. Some scientists recommend that the average person drink about 8 eight-ounce cups of water per day. At this rate, about how many cups of water would a person drink in 2 weeks?

   About _____ cups

3. On average, Americans eat about 20 pounds of pasta per year.

   a. Does this 20 pounds per year seem reasonable to you? _____

      Explain. _____

      _____

   b. At this rate, about how many pounds of pasta would an American eat in 23 years?

      About _____ pounds

      Source: Sicilian Culture, www.sicilianculture.com/food/pasta.htm

4. Thirty-six buses would be needed to carry the passengers and crew of three 747 jumbo jets.

   a. Fill in the rate table.

Buses			36	180	252
Jets	1	2	3		

   b. How many jets would be needed to carry the passengers on 264 buses? _____

5. A man in India grew one of his thumbnails until it was 114 centimeters long. Fingernails grow about 2.5 centimeters each year. At this rate, about how many years did it take the man in India to grow his thumbnail?

   About _____ years

Number Sense **3.0**; Mathematical Reasoning 3.3

LESSON 12·6 **Math Boxes**

---

1. a. Complete the table.

Number of Days	365			
Number of Years	1	2	9	12

b. How many days are in 92 years? _____ days

SRB 47

---

2. Give 3 other names for each measure.

a. 1 gal

_____ _____ _____

b. 1 qt

_____ _____ _____

c. 1 pt

_____ _____ _____

SRB 137

---

3. Find the solution of each open sentence.

a. $y + (-8) = -23$ $y =$ _____

b. $12 + j = -5$ $j =$ _____

c. $35 + r = 25$ $r =$ _____

d. $c + (-115) = -144$ $c =$ _____

SRB 148

---

4. Complete the name-collection box.

2.75

SRB 149

---

5. How likely is it that Raj will pick a 3 of clubs from a regular deck of playing cards without looking? Fill in the circle next to the best answer.

Ⓐ impossible

Ⓑ very unlikely

Ⓒ unlikely

Ⓓ very likely

SRB 80

---

6. Calculate.

a. 10% of 860 = _____

b. 5% of 220 = _____

c. 75% of _____ = 12

d. _____% of 87 = 43.5

e. _____% of 60 = 18

f. _____% of 145 = 36.25

SRB 38 39

LESSON 12·7 **Math Boxes**

---

1. Multiply. Show your work.

$79 * 405 =$ _____

SRB
18 19

---

2. a. Complete the table.

Number of Inches				144	192	324
Number of Feet	1	2	9	12		

b. How many inches are in 11 feet?

_____ inches

SRB
47

---

3. It is estimated that in an average lifetime of 75 years, a person takes about 50,000 trips in a car.

a. At that rate, about how many times a day would a person ride in a car?

_____ times

b. Does this number make sense to you?

_____

SRB
47

---

4. Subtract.

a. $-\$75 - (+\$25) =$ _____

b. $-\$45 - (-\$30) =$ _____

c. $-\$60 - (+\$60) =$ _____

d. $\$55 - (-\$25) =$ _____

e. $\$300 - (-\$100) =$ _____

SRB
60

---

5. Calculate the volume.

3 cm
12 cm
5.5 cm

Number model: _____

Volume = _____ cm³

SRB
138

---

6. A 10-ounce can of peas costs $0.55. A 16-ounce can of peas costs $1.19.

a. What is the price per ounce for each can? (Round to the nearest cent.)

10-oz can: _____

16-oz can: _____

b. Which can of peas is the better buy?

_____

SRB
47

---

1) NS 3.2   2) MR 3.3   3) MR 3.1
4) AF 1.2   5) AF 1.4   6) MR 3.3

My Route Log

Date	Country	Capital	Air distance from last capital	Total distance traveled so far
	1 U.S.A.	Washington, D.C.		
	2 Egypt	Cairo		
	3			
	4			
	5			
	6			
	7			
	8			
	9			
	10			
	11			
	12			
	13			
	14			
	15			
	16			
	17			
	18			
	19			
	20			

Route Map

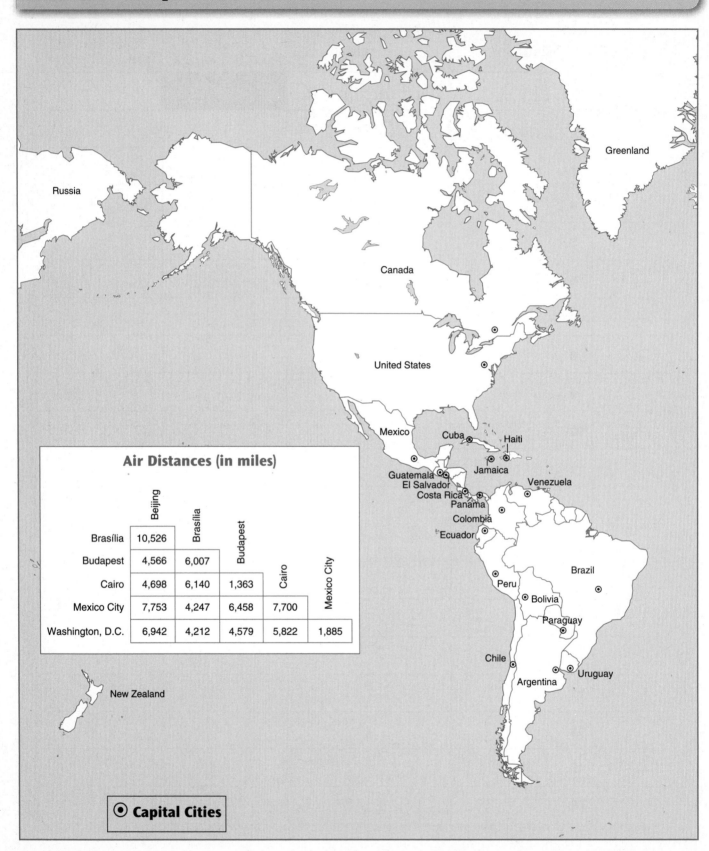

Air Distances (in miles)

	Beijing	Brasília	Budapest	Cairo	Mexico City
Brasília	10,526				
Budapest	4,566	6,007			
Cairo	4,698	6,140	1,363		
Mexico City	7,753	4,247	6,458	7,700	
Washington, D.C.	6,942	4,212	4,579	5,822	1,885

⊙ **Capital Cities**

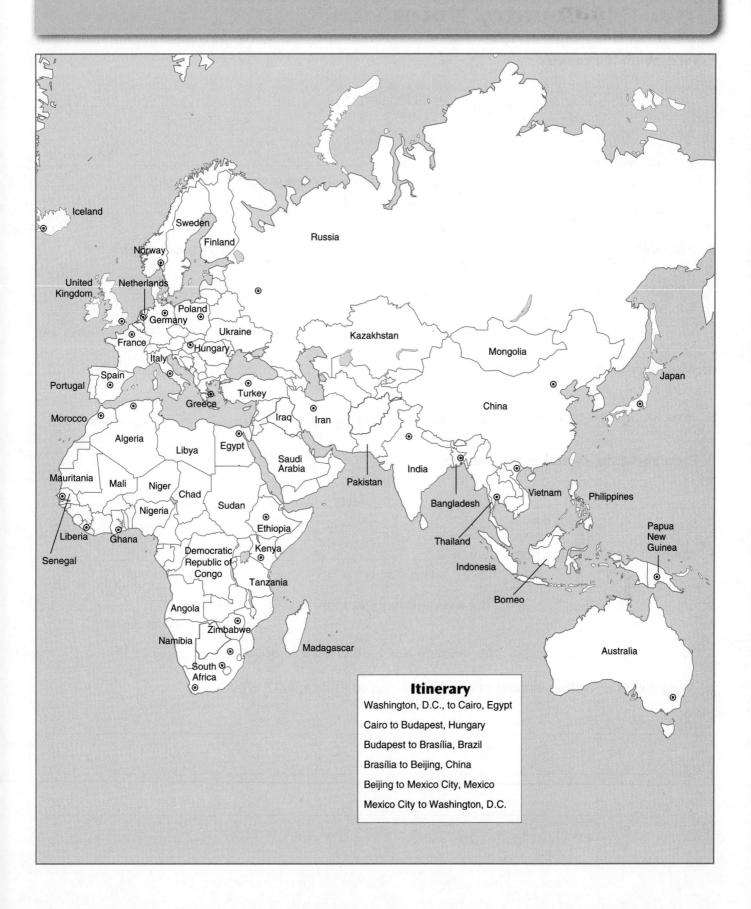

Itinerary

Washington, D.C., to Cairo, Egypt

Cairo to Budapest, Hungary

Budapest to Brasília, Brazil

Brasília to Beijing, China

Beijing to Mexico City, Mexico

Mexico City to Washington, D.C.

LESSON 7·2 My Country Notes

A. Facts about the country

_____ is located in _____.
       name of country   name of continent

1. It is bordered by _____
                                    countries, bodies of water

_____.

2. Population: _____   Area: _____ square miles

3. Languages spoken: _____

_____

4. Monetary unit: _____

5. Exchange rate (optional): 1 _____ = _____

B. Facts about the capital of the country

_____ Population: _____
       name of capital

1. When it is noon in my hometown, it is _____ in _____.
                                          time (A.M. or P.M.?)   name of capital

2. In _____/_____, the average high temperature in _____
     month   month   name of capital

is about _____°F. The average low temperature is about _____°F.

3. What kinds of clothes should I pack for my visit to this capital? Why?

_____

_____

_____

_____

LESSON 7·2

My Country Notes *continued*

4. Turn to the Route Map found on journal pages 330 and 331.
   Draw a line from the last city you visited to the capital of this country.

5. If your class is using the Route Log, record the information on journal page 329 or *Math Masters,* page 421.

6. Can you find any facts on pages 302–305 in your *Student Reference Book* that apply to this country? For example, is one of the 10 tallest mountains in the world located in this country? List all the facts you can find.

_____

_____

_____

_____

C. My impressions about the country

Do you know anyone who has visited or lived in this country? If so, ask that person for an interview. Read about the country's customs and about interesting places to visit there. Use encyclopedias, travel books, the travel section of a newspaper, or library books. Try to get brochures from a travel agent. Then describe below some interesting things you have learned about this country.

_____

_____

_____

_____

_____

_____

_____

My Country Notes

A. Facts about the country

_____ is located in _____.
name of country name of continent

1. It is bordered by _____
countries, bodies of water

_____.

2. Population: _____   Area: _____ square miles

3. Languages spoken: _____

_____

4. Monetary unit: _____

5. Exchange rate (optional): 1 _____ = _____

B. Facts about the capital of the country

_____   Population: _____
name of capital

1. When it is noon in my hometown, it is _____ in _____.
time (A.M. or P.M.?)   name of capital

2. In _____/_____, the average high temperature in _____
month   month   name of capital

is about _____°F. The average low temperature is about _____°F.

3. What kinds of clothes should I pack for my visit to this capital? Why?

_____

_____

_____

_____

4. Turn to the Route Map found on journal pages 330 and 331.
Draw a line from the last city you visited to the capital of this country.

5. If your class is using the Route Log, record the information on journal page 329 or
Math Masters, page 421.

6. Can you find any facts on pages 302–305 in your *Student Reference Book* that
apply to this country? For example, is one of the 10 tallest mountains in the world
located in this country? List all the facts you can find.

_____

_____

_____

_____

C. My impressions about the country

Do you know anyone who has visited or lived in this country? If so, ask that person
for an interview. Read about the country's customs and about interesting places to
visit there. Use encyclopedias, travel books, the travel section of a newspaper, or
library books. Try to get brochures from a travel agent. Then describe below some
interesting things you have learned about this country.

_____

_____

_____

_____

_____

_____

My Country Notes

A. Facts about the country

_____ is located in _____.
name of country   name of continent

1. It is bordered by _____
                        countries, bodies of water

_____.

2. Population: _____   Area: _____ square miles

3. Languages spoken: _____

_____

4. Monetary unit: _____

5. Exchange rate (optional): 1 _____ = _____

B. Facts about the capital of the country

_____ Population: _____
name of capital

1. When it is noon in my hometown, it is _____ in _____.
                            time (A.M. or P.M.?)   name of capital

2. In _____/_____, the average high temperature in _____
     month   month   name of capital

is about _____°F. The average low temperature is about _____°F.

3. What kinds of clothes should I pack for my visit to this capital? Why?

_____

_____

_____

_____

LESSON 9·5 **My Country Notes** *continued*

4. Turn to the Route Map found on journal pages 330 and 331.
Draw a line from the last city you visited to the capital of this country.

5. If your class is using the Route Log, record the information on journal page 329 or *Math Masters,* page 421.

6. Can you find any facts on pages 302–305 in your *Student Reference Book* that apply to this country? For example, is one of the 10 tallest mountains in the world located in this country? List all the facts you can find.

_____

_____

_____

_____

c. **My impressions about the country**

Do you know anyone who has visited or lived in this country? If so, ask that person for an interview. Read about the country's customs and about interesting places to visit there. Use encyclopedias, travel books, the travel section of a newspaper, or library books. Try to get brochures from a travel agent. Then describe below some interesting things you have learned about this country.

_____

_____

_____

_____

_____

_____

LESSON 10·3   My Country Notes

A. Facts about the country

_____ is located in _____ .
name of country   name of continent

1. It is bordered by _____
countries, bodies of water

_____ .

2. Population: _____   Area: _____ square miles

3. Languages spoken: _____

_____

4. Monetary unit: _____

5. Exchange rate (optional): 1 _____ = _____

B. Facts about the capital of the country

_____   Population: _____
name of capital

1. When it is noon in my hometown, it is _____ in _____ .
time (A.M. or P.M.?)   name of capital

2. In _____/_____, the average high temperature in _____
month   month   name of capital

is about _____°F. The average low temperature is about _____°F.

3. What kinds of clothes should I pack for my visit to this capital? Why?

_____

_____

_____

_____

LESSON 10·3 **My Country Notes** *continued*

4. Turn to the Route Map found on journal pages 330 and 331.
   Draw a line from the last city you visited to the capital of this country.

5. If your class is using the Route Log, record the information on journal page 329 or
   Math Masters, page 421.

6. Can you find any facts on pages 302–305 in your *Student Reference Book* that
   apply to this country? For example, is one of the 10 tallest mountains in the world
   located in this country? List all the facts you can find.

_____

_____

_____

_____

_____

C. My impressions about the country

Do you know anyone who has visited or lived in this country? If so, ask that person
for an interview. Read about the country's customs and about interesting places to
visit there. Use encyclopedias, travel books, the travel section of a newspaper, or
library books. Try to get brochures from a travel agent. Then describe below some
interesting things you have learned about this country.

_____

_____

_____

_____

_____

_____

_____

LESSON 11·1 My Country Notes

A. Facts about the country

_____ is located in _____.
name of country   name of continent

1. It is bordered by _____
                                      countries, bodies of water

_____.

2. Population: _____   Area: _____ square miles

3. Languages spoken: _____

_____

4. Monetary unit: _____

5. Exchange rate (optional): 1 _____ = _____

B. Facts about the capital of the country

_____   Population: _____
name of capital

1. When it is noon in my hometown, it is _____ in _____.
                                    time (A.M. or P.M.?)   name of capital

2. In _____/_____, the average high temperature in _____
      month   month   name of capital

is about _____°F. The average low temperature is about _____°F.

3. What kinds of clothes should I pack for my visit to this capital? Why?

_____

_____

_____

_____

LESSON 11·1 My Country Notes continued

4. Turn to the Route Map found on journal pages 330 and 331.
   Draw a line from the last city you visited to the capital of this country.

5. If your class is using the Route Log, record the information on journal page 329 or *Math Masters,* page 421.

6. Can you find any facts on pages 302–305 in your *Student Reference Book* that apply to this country? For example, is one of the 10 tallest mountains in the world located in this country? List all the facts you can find.

_____

_____

_____

_____

_____

c. My impressions about the country

Do you know anyone who has visited or lived in this country? If so, ask that person for an interview. Read about the country's customs and about interesting places to visit there. Use encyclopedias, travel books, the travel section of a newspaper, or library books. Try to get brochures from a travel agent. Then describe below some interesting things you have learned about this country.

_____

_____

_____

_____

_____

_____

_____

Equivalent Names for Fractions

Fraction	Equivalent Fractions	Decimal	Percent
$\frac{0}{2}$		0	0%
$\frac{1}{2}$	$\frac{2}{4}$, $\frac{3}{6}$		
$\frac{2}{2}$		1	100%
$\frac{1}{3}$			
$\frac{2}{3}$			
$\frac{1}{4}$			
$\frac{3}{4}$			
$\frac{1}{5}$			
$\frac{2}{5}$			
$\frac{3}{5}$			
$\frac{4}{5}$			
$\frac{1}{6}$			
$\frac{5}{6}$			
$\frac{1}{8}$			
$\frac{3}{8}$			
$\frac{5}{8}$			
$\frac{7}{8}$			

Number Sense 1.5; Number Sense 1.6

Equivalent Names for Fractions *continued*

Fraction	Equivalent Fractions	Decimal	Percent
$\frac{1}{9}$			
$\frac{2}{9}$			
$\frac{4}{9}$			
$\frac{5}{9}$			
$\frac{7}{9}$			
$\frac{8}{9}$			
$\frac{1}{10}$			
$\frac{3}{10}$			
$\frac{7}{10}$			
$\frac{9}{10}$			
$\frac{1}{12}$			
$\frac{5}{12}$			
$\frac{7}{12}$			
$\frac{11}{12}$			

Number Sense 1.5; Number Sense 1.6

Contents

California Projects

PROJECT 8

Speed and Distance

Math Message

The gray whale is the state marine mammal of California. The name *gray whale* comes from the white marks found on its dark exterior. Gray whales eat small crustaceans. An average gray whale is about 30–50 feet long and can weigh as much as 35 tons.

1. During migration, the average gray whale can travel at a **speed** of 100 miles per day. For a gray whale traveling at 100 miles per day, you can use the following rule to calculate the distance traveled for any number of days:

   Distance traveled = 100 ∗ number of days
   or
   $d = 100 * t$

   where *d* stands for the distance traveled and *t* for the time of travel, in days. For example, after 1 day, the whale will have traveled 100 miles (100 ∗ 1). After 2 days, it will have traveled 200 miles (100 ∗ 2).

2. Use the rule $d = 100 * t$ to complete the table at the right.

Time (days) (t)	Distance (mi) (100 * t)
1	100
2	200
3	
4	
5	
6	
7	
8	
9	
10	

PROJECT 8

Speed and Distance *continued*

3. Complete the graph using the data in the table on page CA2. Then use a straightedge to connect the dots.

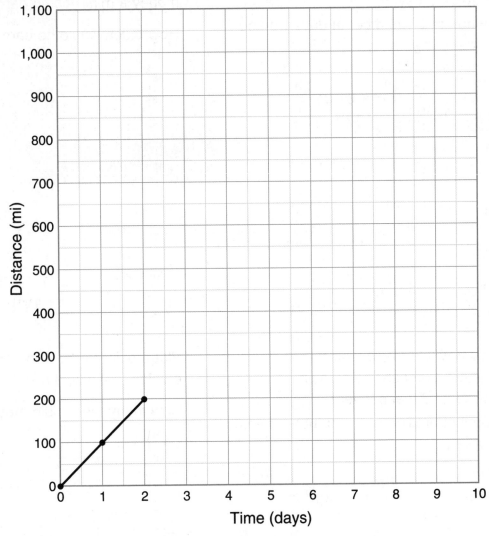

Use your graph to answer the following questions:

4. How far will the gray whale travel in 6 days?   _____ miles

5. How far will the gray whale travel in $2\frac{1}{2}$ days?   _____ miles

6. How many days will it take the gray whale
   to travel 700 miles?   _____ days

7. How many days will it take the gray whale
   to travel 450 miles?   _____ days

Date _____   Time _____

Complete each table below. Then graph the data and connect the points.

1. a. The average miner during the California Gold Rush earned $2 a day.

Rule: Earnings = 2 ∗ number of days worked

Equation: $E = 2 * d$

Time (days) (d)	Earnings ($) (2 ∗ d)
1	
2	
3	
	14
$8\frac{1}{2}$	

b. Plot a point to show the amount of money a miner could earn in 5 days.

How much would he earn? $_____

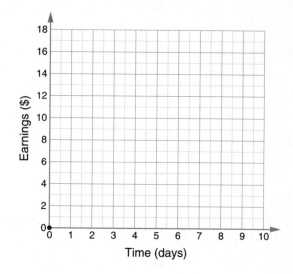

2. a. In Monterey Bay, California, some sand dunes are experiencing erosion at a rate of about 6 feet per year.

Rule: Amount of erosion = 6 ∗ number of years

Equation: $E = 6 * y$

Time (years) (y)	Erosion (feet) (6 ∗ y)
1	
2	
3	
	24
$6\frac{1}{2}$	

b. Plot a point to show the amount of erosion that would result after 8 years.

How many feet would erode? _____ ft

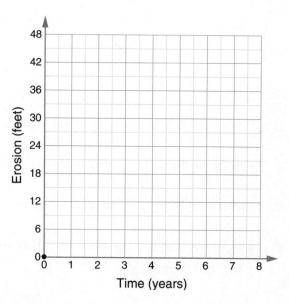

Algebra and Functions **1.5**; Measurement and Geometry **2.0**; Measurement and Geometry **2.1**

PROJECT 8

Representing Rates *continued*

3. a. A tub of sorted, cleaned, bunched, and packaged California grapes holds about 25 pounds.

Rule: Weight = 25 * number of tubs

Equation: $w = 25 * t$

Tubs (t)	Weight (lb) (25 * t)
1	
2	
3	
	14
8	

b. Plot a point to show the approximate weight of 5 tubs of grapes.

How much do they weigh? _____ pounds

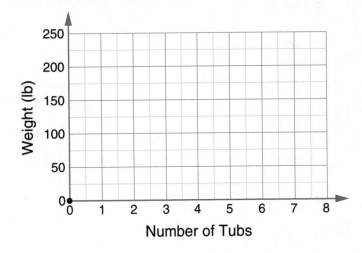

4. a. An average California avocado tree produces about 120 avocados per year.

Rule: Avocados = 120 * number of years

Equation: $a = 120 * y$

Time (years) (y)	Avocados (120 * y)
	120
$1\frac{1}{2}$	
2	
$3\frac{1}{2}$	
	600

b. Plot a point to show the number of avocados produced by an average tree in 4 years.

How many avocados would be produced? _____ avocados

PROJECT 9 **Coordinate Grid Distances**

1. Plot and label the following points on the coordinate grid.

A   (0,8)

B   (5,8)

C   (9,3)

D   (9,10)

E   (7,0)

F   (7,6)

G   (1,3)

H   (4,3)

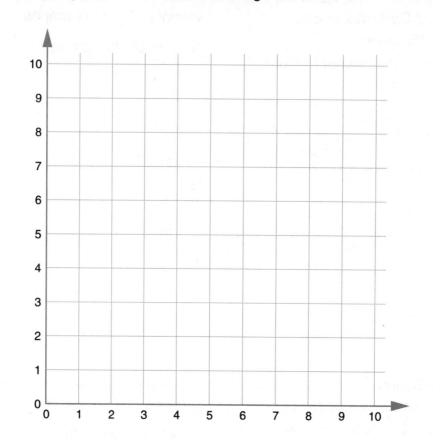

Use a straightedge to complete Problems 2–5.

2. Draw a line segment to connect points A and B.

   The length of $\overline{AB}$ is _____ units.

3. Draw a line segment to connect points C and D.

   The length of $\overline{CD}$ is _____ units.

4. Draw a line segment to connect points E and F.

   The length of $\overline{EF}$ is _____ units.

5. Draw a line segment to connect points G and H.

   The length of $\overline{GH}$ is _____ units.

Measurement and Geometry **2.0**; Measurement and Geometry **2.2**; Measurement and Geometry **2.3**

PROJECT 9 **Coordinate Grid Distances** *continued*

6. Find the length of the line segment connecting the points.

   a. (3,5) and (7,5) _____ units   **b.** (4,10) and (9,10) _____ units

   c. (8,12) and (8,1) _____ units   **d.** (10,15) and (5,15) _____ units

   e. (7,24) and (7,39) _____ units   **f.** (6,26) and (6,43) _____ units

   g. $(6\frac{1}{2},9)$ and (2,9) _____ units   **h.** $(3,5\frac{1}{4})$ and (3,7) _____ units

7. Name two ordered-number pairs. The points should lie on the same horizontal line segment. Find the length of the line segment connecting the points.

   a. (___,___) and (___,___)   _____ units

   b. (___,___) and (___,___)   _____ units

   c. (___,___) and (___,___)   _____ units

8. Name two ordered-number pairs. The points should lie on the same vertical line segment. Find the length of the line segment connecting the points.

   a. (___,___) and (___,___)   _____ units

   b. (___,___) and (___,___)   _____ units

   c. (___,___) and (___,___)   _____ units

PROJECT 9

Coordinate Grid Distances *continued*

CALIFORNIA

9. How is finding the length of a horizontal line segment on a coordinate grid without counting similar to finding the length of a vertical line segment without counting? How is it different?

_____

_____

_____

_____

Use *Student Reference Book* page CA12 to help you solve Problems 10–12.

10. Katrina walked from the concert hall to Ronald Reagan State Building. She walked the shortest possible distance along the city streets. How many blocks did she walk?   _____ blocks

11. Marco walked from the athletic club to Los Angeles Central Library. Then he walked to Biddy Mason Park. He walked the shortest possible distance along the city streets. How many blocks did he walk in all?   _____ blocks

12. Make up a "walking" problem of your own. Ask a partner to solve it.

_____

_____

_____

_____

Answer: _____ blocks

Try This

13. Gabriel drew a vertical line segment on a coordinate grid. The line segment is 4 units long. One of the endpoints is (7,6). What is the other endpoint? Give all possible solutions.

_____

PROJECT 10

Properties of Equality

Addition Property of Equality	Multiplication Property of Equality
Equals added to equals are equal.	Equals multiplied by equals are equal.
You know 3 + 4 = 7.	You know 13 = 5 + 8.
So, 3 + 4 + 10 = 7 + 10.	So, 13 * 2 = (5 + 8) * 2.

1. For each pan balance, draw the objects that will make the pans equally balanced.

a.

b.

c.

2. For each pan balance, write the number that will make the sides of the pan balance equal.

a.

21 + 13

b.

13 − 8

c.

(4 * 8) + 6

PROJECT 10 **Properties of Equality** *continued*

3. The shaded box shows what has been added to each equation. Write an operation symbol and a number in each blank box to make both sides of the equation equal.

a. $24 - 5$ $\boxed{+ 3}$ $= 19$ $\boxed{}$

b. 16 $\boxed{}$ $= 10 + 6$ $\boxed{+ 7}$

c. $10 + 29$ $\boxed{+ 4}$ $= 39$ $\boxed{}$

d. $(12 * 4)$ $\boxed{+ 5}$ $= 48$ $\boxed{}$

4. Write an operation symbol and a number in each box to complete the equation.

a. 4 $\boxed{}$ $= 9 - 5 + 8$

b. $(35 \div 7) + 8 = 5$ $\boxed{}$

c. $9h$ $\boxed{}$ $= 9h + 3$

d. $4 + (w + 2) =$ $\boxed{}$ $(w + 2)$

5. The equation $81 \div 9 = 9$ is balanced. Vidur said the equation $(81 \div 9) + 5 = 9 - 5$ is also balanced. Do you agree? Explain your answer.

_____

_____

_____

_____

6. The equation $15 + 3 = 18$ is balanced. Anika said the equation $(15 + 3) + 6 = 18 + 6$ is also balanced. Do you agree? Explain your answer.

_____

_____

_____

_____

PROJECT 10 **Properties of Equality** *continued*

7. The shaded box shows what has been added to each equation. Write an operation symbol and a number in each blank box to make both sides of the equation equal.

a. (40 ÷ 5) [* 7] = 8 [   ]

b. [5 *] (7 + 6) = 13 [   ]

c. (5 * 7) [* 9] = 35 [   ]

d. (23 − 12) [   ] = 11 [* 6]

8. Write an operation symbol and a number in each box to complete the equation.

a. (10 ÷ 5) * 3 = 2 [   ]

b. (10 * 13) [   ] = 130 * 8

c. 4y * 10 = 4y [   ]

d. 8 * (m − 3) = [   ] (m − 3)

9. The equation 18 − 9 = 9 is balanced. Juhi said the equation (18 − 9) * **10** = 9 * **10** is also balanced. Do you agree? Explain your answer.

_____

_____

_____

_____

10. The equation 25 ÷ 5 = 5 is balanced. Ethan said the equation **6** * (25 ÷ 5) = **6** + 5 is also balanced. Do you agree? Explain your answer.

_____

_____

_____

_____

PROJECT 11

One-Digit Divisors

1. The fourth-grade classes at Glendale School put on puppet shows
   for their families and friends. Ticket sales totaled $532, which the
   four classes are to share equally. How much should each class get?   _____

   Be ready to explain how you found your answer.

2. 78 / 6 = _____   3. 288 / 8 = _____

4. _____ = 564 / 3   5. _____ = 763 / 7

PROJECT 11

One-Digit Divisors *continued*

6. 350 / 4 = _____

7. 802 / 9 = _____

8. _____ = 869 / 7

9. _____ = 874 / 5

One-Digit Divisors *continued*

10. Eight people visited a marine theme park in San Diego. The total cost of the single-day admission tickets was $424. What was the cost per ticket?

_____

11. Muir Woods National Monument charges an entrance fee of $3 per person. A school group visited the site. The cost was $288. How many people were in the school group?

_____ people

12. Six tourists took a ferry to visit Alcatraz in the middle of San Francisco Bay. The total cost of the trip was $99. What was the price of each ticket?

_____

13. Four friends spent the day at an amusement park in Los Angeles. The total cost of the tickets was $299.96. What was the price per ticket?

_____

Date _____   Time _____

1. Four friends were playing a board game. Jen quit. The three other players decided to divide Jen's money equally. Jen had $4,353. How much should each of the three other players get?   _____

   Be ready to explain how you got your answer.

2. $5,385 / 5 = _____

3. $7,896 / 6 = _____

4. _____ = 8,575 / 7

5. _____ = 8,127 / 3

PROJECT 12

Larger Dividends *continued*

Fill in the missing numbers.

6.

```
    1 □ 3 9
 5) 8 6 9 5
  - 5
    3 6
  - 3 5
      □ 9
    - 1 5
        4 □
      - 4 5
          0
```

7.

```
      0 5 □ □
   6) 3 2 5 2
    - 0
      3 2
    - □ 0
        2 □
      - 2 4
          1 2
        - 1 □
            0
```

8. The total cost for one year (2006-2007) at University of California, Los Angeles (UCLA) is about $23,394 for a California resident living in a residence hall. Books and supplies account for about $1,544 of the total cost.

a. How many hours of babysitting at $4 per hour would it take to earn $1,544?

_____ hours

b. How many hours of babysitting at $6 per hour would it take to earn $23,394?

_____ hours

Number Sense **3.2**; Number Sense **3.4**

PROJECT 12 **Dividing Dollars and Cents**

1. Dennis solved $9.45 / 7 like this.

   a. Study Dennis's work.

   b. Explain to your partner how he
   solved the problem.

$$
\begin{array}{r}
1.35 \\
7\overline{)9.45} \\
-7 \\
\hline
24 \\
-21 \\
\hline
35 \\
-35 \\
\hline
0
\end{array}
$$

Solve these division problems using Dennis's method.

2. $8.92 / 4 = _____

3. $7.56 / 6 = _____

4. _____ = 15.76 / 8

5. _____ = 19.17 / 9

California Content Standards

The California Mathematics Content Standards describe what every child in California can and needs to learn in mathematics. These standards are identified at the bottom of each of your journal pages and are listed here for your reference. The oval identifies the key standards for this grade level.

Page 185

Number Sense 1.5 Explain different interpretations of fractions, for example, parts of a whole, parts of a set, and division of whole numbers by whole numbers; explain equivalents of fractions (see Standard 4.0).

Number Sense 1.7 Write the fraction represented by a drawing of parts of a figure; represent a given fraction by using drawings; and relate a fraction to a simple decimal on a number line.

Page 186

Number Sense 1.5 Explain different interpretations of fractions, for example, parts of a whole, parts of a set, and division of whole numbers by whole numbers; explain equivalents of fractions (see Standard 4.0).

Mathematical Reasoning 2.3 Use a variety of methods, such as words, numbers, symbols, charts, graphs, tables, diagrams, and models, to explain mathematical reasoning.

Page 187

Number Sense 1.5 Explain different interpretations of fractions, for example, parts of a whole, parts of a set, and division of whole numbers by whole numbers; explain equivalents of fractions (see Standard 4.0).

Number Sense (1.9) Identify on a number line the relative position of positive fractions, positive mixed numbers, and positive decimals to two decimal places.

Pages 189, 190

Number Sense 1.7 Write the fraction represented by a drawing of parts of a figure; represent a given fraction by using drawings; and relate a fraction to a simple decimal on a number line.

Number Sense 1.5 Explain different interpretations of fractions, for example, parts of a whole, parts of a set, and division of whole numbers by whole numbers; explain equivalents of fractions (see Standard 4.0).

Page 192

Statistics, Data Analysis, and Probability 2.1 Represent all possible outcomes for a simple probability situation in an organized way (e.g., tables, grids, tree diagrams).

Statistics, Data Analysis, and Probability 2.2 Express outcomes of experimental probability situations verbally and numerically (e.g., 3 out of 4; $\frac{3}{4}$).

Pages 194, 195

Number Sense 1.5 Explain different interpretations of fractions, for example, parts of a whole, parts of a set, and division of whole numbers by whole numbers; explain equivalents of fractions (see Standard 4.0).

Number Sense 1.7 Write the fraction represented by a drawing of parts of a figure; represent a given fraction by using drawings; and relate a fraction to a simple decimal on a number line.

Measurement and Geometry 3.0 Students demonstrate an understanding of plane and solid geometric objects and use this knowledge to show relationships and solve problems.

Page 196

Number Sense 1.5 Explain different interpretations of fractions, for example, parts of a whole, parts of a set, and division of whole numbers by whole numbers; explain equivalents of fractions (see Standard 4.0).

Number Sense 1.7 Write the fraction represented by a drawing of parts of a figure; represent a given fraction by using drawings; and relate a fraction to a simple decimal on a number line.

Measurement and Geometry 3.0 Students demonstrate an understanding of plane and solid geometric objects and use this knowledge to show relationships and solve problems.

Mathematical Reasoning 2.2 Apply strategies and results from simpler problems to more complex problems.

Page 198

Number Sense 1.5 Explain different interpretations of fractions, for example, parts of a whole, parts of a set, and division of whole numbers by whole numbers; explain equivalents of fractions (see Standard 4.0).

Measurement and Geometry 3.0 Students demonstrate an understanding of plane and solid geometric objects and use this knowledge to show relationships and solve problems.

Number Sense 1.7 Write the fraction represented by a drawing of parts of a figure; represent a given fraction by using drawings; and relate a fraction to a simple decimal on a number line.

Page 201

Number Sense 1.5 Explain different interpretations of fractions, for example, parts of a whole, parts of a set, and division of whole numbers by whole numbers; explain equivalents of fractions (see Standard 4.0).

Mathematical Reasoning 3.3 Develop generalizations of the results obtained and apply them in other circumstances.

Number Sense 1.7 Write the fraction represented by a drawing of parts of a figure; represent a given fraction by using drawings; and relate a fraction to a simple decimal on a number line.

Page 203

Number Sense 1.6 Write tenths and hundredths in decimal and fraction notations and know the fraction and decimal equivalents for halves and fourths (e.g., $\frac{1}{2}$ = 0.5 or .50; $\frac{7}{4}$ = $1\frac{3}{4}$ = 1.75).

Page 205

Number Sense 1.5 Explain different interpretations of fractions, for example, parts of a whole, parts of a set, and division of whole numbers by whole numbers; explain equivalents of fractions (see Standard 4.0).

Page 206

Number Sense (1.9) Identify on a number line the relative position of positive fractions, positive mixed numbers, and positive decimals to two decimal places.

Page 208

Number Sense 1.5 Explain different interpretations of fractions, for example, parts of a whole, parts of a set, and division of whole numbers by whole numbers; explain equivalents of fractions (see Standard 4.0).

Number Sense 1.7 Write the fraction represented by a drawing of parts of a figure; represent a given fraction by using drawings; and relate a fraction to a simple decimal on a number line.

Measurement and Geometry 3.0 Students demonstrate an understanding of plane and solid geometric objects and use this knowledge to show relationships and solve problems.

Page 209

Number Sense 1.5 Explain different interpretations of fractions, for example, parts of a whole, parts of a set, and division of whole numbers by whole numbers; explain equivalents of fractions (see Standard 4.0).

Number Sense 1.7 Write the fraction represented by a drawing of parts of a figure; represent a given fraction by using drawings; and relate a fraction to a simple decimal on a number line.

Page 211

Statistics, Data Analysis, and Probability 2.2 Express outcomes of experimental probability situations verbally and numerically (e.g., 3 out of 4; $\frac{3}{4}$).

Page 213

Statistics, Data Analysis, and Probability 2.1 Represent all possible outcomes for a simple probability situation in an organized way (e.g., tables, grids, tree diagrams).

Statistics, Data Analysis, and Probability 2.2 Express outcomes of experimental probability situations verbally and numerically (e.g., 3 out of 4; $\frac{3}{4}$).

Pages 214, 215

Statistics, Data Analysis, and Probability 2.2 Express outcomes of experimental probability situations verbally and numerically (e.g., 3 out of 4; $\frac{3}{4}$).

Statistics, Data Analysis, and Probability 2.1 Represent all possible outcomes for a simple probability situation in an organized way (e.g. tables, grids, tree diagrams).

Number Sense 1.6 Write tenths and hundredths in decimal and fraction notations and know the fraction and decimal equivalents for halves and fourths (e.g., $\frac{1}{2}$ = 0.5 or .50; $\frac{7}{4}$ = $1\frac{3}{4}$ = 1.75).

Page 216

Number Sense 1.0 Students understand the place value of whole numbers and decimals to two decimal places and how whole numbers and decimals relate to simple fractions. Students use the concepts of negative numbers.

Number Sense 1.2 Order and compare whole numbers and decimals to two decimal places.

Pages 219, 220

Measurement and Geometry 1.0 Students understand perimeter and area.

Measurement and Geometry 1.4 Understand and use formulas to solve problems involving perimeters and areas of rectangles and squares. Use those formulas to find the areas of more complex figures by dividing the figures into basic shapes.

Page 221

Measurement and Geometry 1.0 Students understand perimeter and area.

Measurement and Geometry 1.4 Understand and use formulas to solve problems involving perimeters and areas of rectangles and squares. Use those formulas to find the areas of more complex figures by dividing the figures into basic shapes.

Statistics, Data Analysis, and Probability 1.2 Identify the mode(s) for sets of categorical data and the mode(s), median, and any apparent outliers for numerical data sets.

Page 222

Measurement and Geometry 1.0 Students understand perimeter and area.

Measurement and Geometry 1.4 Understand and use formulas to solve problems involving perimeters and areas of rectangles and squares. Use those formulas to find the areas of more complex figures by dividing the figures into basic shapes.

Pages 224, 225

Measurement and Geometry 1.0 Students understand perimeter and area.

Measurement and Geometry 1.1 Measure the area of rectangular shapes by using appropriate units, such as square centimeter (cm²), square meter (m²), square kilometer (km²), square inch (in²), square yard (yd²), or square mile (mi²).

Page 227

Measurement and Geometry 1.0 Students understand perimeter and area.

Measurement and Geometry 1.1 Measure the area of rectangular shapes by using appropriate units, such as square centimeter (cm²), square meter (m²), square kilometer (km²), square inch (in²), square yard (yd²), or square mile (mi²).

Page 230

Measurement and Geometry 1.0 Students understand perimeter and area.

Mathematical Reasoning 2.2 Apply strategies and results from simpler problems to more complex problems.

Mathematical Reasoning 2.5 Indicate the relative advantages of exact and approximate solutions to problems and give answers to a specified degree of accuracy.

Page 231

Measurement and Geometry 1.1 Measure the area of rectangular shapes by using appropriate units, such as square centimeter (cm²), square meter (m²), square kilometer (km²), square inch (in²), square yard (yd²), or square mile (mi²).

Page 232

Measurement and Geometry 1.1 Measure the area of rectangular shapes by using appropriate units, such as square centimeter (cm²), square meter (m²), square kilometer (km²), square inch (in²), square yard (yd²), or square mile (mi²).

Measurement and Geometry 1.4 Understand and use formulas to solve problems involving perimeters and areas of rectangles and squares. Use those formulas to find the areas of more complex figures by dividing the figures into basic shapes.

Algebra and Functions 1.1 Use letters, boxes, or other symbols to stand for any number in simple expressions or equations (e.g., demonstrate an understanding and the use of the concept of a variable).

Algebra and Functions 1.4 Use and interpret formulas (e.g., area = length × width or A = lw) to answer questions about quantities and their relationships.

Mathematical Reasoning 1.1 Analyze problems by identifying relationships, distinguishing relevant from irrelevant information, sequencing and prioritizing information, and observing patterns.

Page 233

Measurement and Geometry 1.1 Measure the area of rectangular shapes by using appropriate units, such as square centimeter (cm²), square meter (m²), square kilometer (km²), square inch (in²), square yard (yd²), or square mile (mi²).

Measurement and Geometry 1.4 Understand and use formulas to solve problems involving perimeters and areas of rectangles and squares. Use those formulas to find the areas of more complex figures by dividing the figures into basic shapes.

Algebra and Functions 1.1 Use letters, boxes, or other symbols to stand for any number in simple expressions or equations (e.g., demonstrate an understanding and the use of the concept of a variable).

Algebra and Functions 1.4 Use and interpret formulas (e.g., area = length × width or A = lw) to answer questions about quantities and their relationships.

Page 234

Measurement and Geometry 2.0 Students use two-dimensional coordinate grids to represent points and graph lines and simple figures.

Measurement and Geometry 2.2 Understand that the length of a horizontal line segment equals the difference of the x-coordinates.

Measurement and Geometry 2.3 Understand that the length of a vertical line segment equals the difference of the y-coordinates.

Page 320

Number Sense 3.3 Solve problems involving multiplication of multidigit numbers by two-digit numbers.

Number Sense 3.4 Solve problems involving division of multidigit numbers by one-digit numbers.

Page 322

Number Sense 3.4 Solve problems involving division of multidigit numbers by one-digit numbers.

Page 324

Number Sense 3.0 Students solve problems involving addition, subtraction, multiplication, and division of whole numbers and understand the relationships among the operations.

Mathematical Reasoning 2.3 Use a variety of methods, such as words, numbers, symbols, charts, graphs, tables, diagrams, and models, to explain mathematical reasoning.

Page 326

Number Sense 3.0 Students solve problems involving addition, subtraction, multiplication, and division of whole numbers and understand the relationships among the operations.

Mathematical Reasoning 3.3 Develop generalizations of the results obtained and apply them in other circumstances.

Pages 342, 343

Number Sense 1.5 Explain different interpretations of fractions, for example, parts of a whole, parts of a set, and division of whole numbers by whole numbers; explain equivalents of fractions (see Standard 4.0).

Number Sense 1.6 Write tenths and hundredths in decimal and fraction notations and know the fraction and decimal equivalents for halves and fourths (e.g., $\frac{1}{2} = 0.5$ or $.50$; $\frac{7}{4} = 1\frac{3}{4} = 1.75$).

Pages CA2–CA5

Algebra and Functions 1.5 Understand that an equation such as $y = 3x \times 5$ is a prescription for determining a second number when a first number is given.

Measurement and Geometry 2.0 Students use two-dimensional coordinate grids to represent points and graph lines and simple figures.

Measurement and Geometry 2.1 Draw the points corresponding to linear relationships on graph paper (e.g., draw 10 points on the graph of the equation $y = 3x$ and connect them by using a straight line).

Pages CA6–CA8

Measurement and Geometry 2.0 Students use two-dimensional coordinate grids to represent points and graph lines and simple figures.

Measurement and Geometry 2.2 Understand that the length of a horizontal line segment equals the difference of the x-coordinates.

Measurement and Geometry 2.3 Understand that the length of a vertical line segment equals the difference of the y-coordinates.

Pages CA9–CA11

Algebra and Functions 2.0 Students know how to manipulate equations.

Algebra and Functions 2.1 Know and understand that equals added to equals are equal.

Algebra and Functions 2.2 Know and understand that equals multiplied by equals are equal.

Pages CA12–CA14

Number Sense 3.2 Demonstrate an understanding of, and the ability to use, standard algorithms for multiplying a multidigit number by a two-digit number and for dividing a multidigit number by a one-digit number; use relationships between them to simplify computations and to check results.

Pages CA15–CA17

Number Sense 3.2 Demonstrate an understanding of, and the ability to use, standard algorithms for multiplying a multidigit number by a two-digit number and for dividing a multidigit number by a one-digit number; use relationships between them to simplify computations and to check results.

Number Sense 3.4 Solve problems involving division of multidigit numbers by one-digit numbers.

California Content Standards for Math Boxes

Math Boxes 7✦1

1. **Number Sense 1.7** Write the fraction represented by a drawing of parts of a figure; represent a given fraction by using drawings; and relate a fraction to a simple decimal on a number line.

2. **Measurement and Geometry 3.5** Know the definitions of a right angle, an acute angle, and an obtuse angle. Understand that 90°, 180°, 270°, and 360° are associated, respectively, with $\frac{1}{4}$, $\frac{1}{2}$, $\frac{3}{4}$, and full turns.

3. **Number Sense 3.2** Demonstrate an understanding of, and the ability to use, standard algorithms for multiplying a multidigit number by a two-digit number and for dividing a multidigit number by a one-digit number; use relationships between them to simplify computations and to check results.

4. **Statistics, Data Analysis, and Probability 1.2** Identify the mode(s. for sets of categorical data and the mode(s), median, and any apparent outliers for numerical data sets.

5. **Mathematical Reasoning 2.0** Students use strategies, skills, and concepts in finding solutions.

6. **Measurement and Geometry 1.0** Students understand perimeter and area.

Math Boxes 7✦2

1. **Number Sense 1.7** Write the fraction represented by a drawing of parts of a figure; represent a given fraction by using drawings; and relate a fraction to a simple decimal on a number line.

2. **Measurement and Geometry 3.5** Know the definitions of a right angle, an acute angle, and an obtuse angle. Understand that 90°, 180°, 270°, and 360° are associated, respectively, with $\frac{1}{4}$, $\frac{1}{2}$, $\frac{3}{4}$, and full turns.

3. **Mathematical Reasoning 2.6** Make precise calculations and check the validity of the results from the context of the problem.

4. **Number Sense 3.2** Demonstrate an understanding of, and the ability to use, standard algorithms for multiplying a multidigit number by a two-digit number and for dividing a multidigit number by a one-digit number; use relationships between them to simplify computations and to check results.

5. **Number Sense 3.3** Solve problems involving multiplication of multidigit numbers by two-digit numbers.

6. **Measurement and Geometry 1.1** Measure the area of rectangular shapes by using appropriate units, such as square centimeter, (cm²), square meter (m²), square kilometer (km²), square inch (in²), square yard (yd²), or square mile (mi²).

Math Boxes 7✦3

1. **Number Sense 1.7** Write the fraction represented by a drawing of parts of a figure; represent a given fraction by using drawings; and relate a fraction to a simple decimal on a number line.

2. **Measurement and Geometry 3.5** Know the definitions of a right angle, an acute angle, and an obtuse angle. Understand that 90°, 180°, 270°, and 360° are associated, respectively, with $\frac{1}{4}$, $\frac{1}{2}$, $\frac{3}{4}$, and full turns.

3. **Number Sense 3.2** Demonstrate an understanding of, and the ability to use, standard algorithms for multiplying a multidigit number by a two-digit number and for dividing a multidigit number by a one-digit number; use relationships between them to simplify computations and to check results.

4. **Statistics, Data Analysis, and Probability 1.2** Identify the mode(s) for sets of categorical data and the mode(s), median, and any apparent outliers for numerical data sets.

5. **Mathematical Reasoning 2.0** Students use strategies, skills, and concepts in finding solutions.

6. **Measurement and Geometry 1.0** Students understand perimeter and area.

Math Boxes 7✦4

1. **Number Sense 1.7** Write the fraction represented by a drawing of parts of a figure; represent a given fraction by using drawings; and relate a fraction to a simple decimal on a number line.

2. **Measurement and Geometry 3.5** Know the definitions of a right angle, an acute angle, and an obtuse angle. Understand that 90°, 180°, 270°, and 360° are associated, respectively, with $\frac{1}{4}$, $\frac{1}{2}$, $\frac{3}{4}$, and full turns.

3. **Mathematical Reasoning 2.6** Make precise calculations and check the validity of the results from the context of the problem.

4. **Number Sense 3.2** Demonstrate an understanding of, and the ability to use, standard algorithms for multiplying a multidigit number by a two-digit number and for dividing a multidigit number by a one-digit number; use relationships between them to simplify computations and to check results.

5. **Number Sense 3.3** Solve problems involving multiplication of multidigit numbers by two-digit numbers.

6. **Measurement and Geometry 1.1** Measure the area of rectangular shapes by using appropriate units, such as square centimeter, (cm²), square meter (m²), square kilometer (km²), square inch (in²), square yard (yd²), or square mile (mi²).

Math Boxes 7✦5

1. **Number Sense 1.7** Write the fraction represented by a drawing of parts of a figure; represent a given fraction by using drawings; and relate a fraction to a simple decimal on a number line.

2. **Algebra and Functions 1.3** Use parentheses to indicate which operation to perform first when writing expressions containing more than two terms and different operations.

3. **Measurement and Geometry 2.0** Students use two-dimensional coordinate grids to represent points and graph lines and simple figures.

4. **Measurement and Geometry 3.5** Know the definitions of a right angle, an acute angle, and an obtuse angle. Understand that 90°, 180°, 270°, and 360° are associated, respectively, with $\frac{1}{4}$, $\frac{1}{2}$, $\frac{3}{4}$, and full turns.

Math Boxes 7◆5 *cont.*

5. Statistics, Data Analysis, and Probability 2.2 Express outcomes of experimental probability situations verbally and numerically (e.g., 3 out of 4; $\frac{3}{4}$).

6. Algebra and Functions 1.4 Use and interpret formulas (e.g., area = length × width or $A = lw$) to answer questions about quantities and their relationships.

Math Boxes 7◆6

1. Number Sense 1.5 Explain different interpretations of fractions, for example, parts of a whole, parts of a set, and division of whole numbers by whole numbers; explain equivalents of fractions (see Standard 4.0).

2. Statistics, Data Analysis, and Probability 2.2 Express outcomes of experimental probability situations verbally and numerically (e.g., 3 out of 4; $\frac{3}{4}$).

3. Mathematical Reasoning 2.3 Use a variety of methods, such as words, numbers, symbols, charts, graphs, tables, diagrams, and models, to explain mathematical reasoning.

4. Measurement and Geometry 3.5 Know the definitions of a right angle, an acute angle, and an obtuse angle. Understand that 90°, 180°, 270°, and 360° are associated, respectively, with $\frac{1}{4}$, $\frac{1}{2}$, $\frac{3}{4}$, and full turns.

5. Mathematical Reasoning 2.6 Make precise calculations and check the validity of the results from the context of the problem.

6. Number Sense 1.4 Decide when a rounded solution is called for and explain why such a solution may be appropriate.

Math Boxes 7◆7

1. Number Sense 1.7 Write the fraction represented by a drawing of parts of a figure; represent a given fraction by using drawings; and relate a fraction to a simple decimal on a number line.

2. Algebra and Functions 1.3 Use parentheses to indicate which operation to perform first when writing expressions containing more than two terms and different operations.

3. Measurement and Geometry 2.0 Students use two-dimensional coordinate grids to represent points and graph lines and simple figures.

4. Measurement and Geometry 3.5 Know the definitions of a right angle, an acute angle, and an obtuse angle. Understand that 90°, 180°, 270°, and 360° are associated, respectively, with $\frac{1}{4}$, $\frac{1}{2}$, $\frac{3}{4}$, and full turns.

5. Statistics, Data Analysis, and Probability 2.2 Express outcomes of experimental probability situations verbally and numerically (e.g., 3 out of 4; $\frac{3}{4}$).

6. Algebra and Functions 1.4 Use and interpret formulas (e.g., area = length × width or $A = lw$) to answer questions about quantities and their relationships.

Math Boxes 7◆8

1. Number Sense 1.5 Explain different interpretations of fractions, for example, parts of a whole, parts of a set, and division of whole numbers by whole numbers; explain equivalents of fractions (see Standard 4.0).

2. Statistics, Data Analysis, and Probability 2.2 Express outcomes of experimental probability situations verbally and numerically (e.g., 3 out of 4; $\frac{3}{4}$).

3. Mathematical Reasoning 2.3 Use a variety of methods, such as words, numbers, symbols, charts, graphs, tables, diagrams, and models, to explain mathematical reasoning.

4. Measurement and Geometry 3.5 Know the definitions of a right angle, an acute angle, and an obtuse angle. Understand that 90°, 180°, 270°, and 360° are associated, respectively, with $\frac{1}{4}$, $\frac{1}{2}$, $\frac{3}{4}$, and full turns.

5. Mathematical Reasoning 2.6 Make precise calculations and check the validity of the results from the context of the problem.

6. Number Sense 1.4 Decide when a rounded solution is called for and explain why such a solution may be appropriate.

Math Boxes 7◆9

1. Mathematical Reasoning 1.2 Determine when and how to break a problem into simpler parts.

2. Number Sense 3.2 Demonstrate an understanding of, and the ability to use, standard algorithms for multiplying a multidigit number by a two-digit number and for dividing a multidigit number by a one-digit number; use relationships between them to simplify computations and to check results.

3. Mathematical Reasoning 1.1 Analyze problems by identifying relationships, distinguishing relevant from irrelevant information, sequencing and prioritizing information, and observing patterns.

4. Number Sense 1.6 Write tenths and hundredths in decimal and fraction notations and know the fraction and decimal equivalents for halves and fourths (e.g., $\frac{1}{2}$ = 0.5 or .50; $\frac{7}{4}$ = $1\frac{3}{4}$ = 1.75).

5. Number Sense 2.0 Students extend their use and understanding of whole numbers to the addition and subtraction of simple decimals.

6. Algebra and Functions 1.5 Understand that an equation such as $y = 3x + 5$ is a prescription for determining a second number when a first number is given.

Math Boxes 7◆10

1. Number Sense 1.6 Write tenths and hundredths in decimal and fraction notations and know the fraction and decimal equivalents for halves and fourths (e.g., $\frac{1}{2}$ = 0.5 or .50; $\frac{7}{4}$ = $1\frac{3}{4}$ = 1.75).

2. Algebra and Functions 1.0 Students use and interpret variables, mathematical symbols, and properties to write and simplify expressions and sentences.

3. Number Sense 1.5 Explain different interpretations of fractions, for example, parts of a whole, parts of a set, and division of whole numbers by whole numbers; explain equivalents of fractions (see Standard 4.0).

Math Boxes 7◆10 cont.

4. **Number Sense** **3.2** Demonstrate an understanding of, and the ability to use, standard algorithms for multiplying a multidigit number by a two-digit number and for dividing a multidigit number by a one-digit number; use relationships between them to simplify computations and to check results.

5. **Number Sense** **3.2** Demonstrate an understanding of, and the ability to use, standard algorithms for multiplying a multidigit number by a two-digit number and for dividing a multidigit number by a one-digit number; use relationships between them to simplify computations and to check results.

6. **Mathematical Reasoning 1.2** Determine when and how to break a problem into simpler parts.

Math Boxes 7◆11

1. **Mathematical Reasoning 1.2** Determine when and how to break a problem into simpler parts.

2. **Number Sense** **3.2** Demonstrate an understanding of, and the ability to use, standard algorithms for multiplying a multidigit number by a two-digit number and for dividing a multidigit number by a one-digit number; use relationships between them to simplify computations and to check results.

3. **Mathematical Reasoning 1.1** Analyze problems by identifying relationships, distinguishing relevant from irrelevant information, sequencing and prioritizing information, and observing patterns.

4. **Number Sense 1.6** Write tenths and hundredths in decimal and fraction notations and know the fraction and decimal equivalents for halves and fourths (e.g., $\frac{1}{2} = 0.5$ or $.50$; $\frac{7}{4} = 1\frac{3}{4} = 1.75$).

5. **Number Sense 2.0** Students extend their use and understanding of whole numbers to the addition and subtraction of simple decimals.

6. **Algebra and Functions** **1.5** Understand that an equation such as $y = 3x + 5$ is a prescription for determining a second number when a first number is given.

Math Boxes 7◆12

1. **Number Sense 1.6** Write tenths and hundredths in decimal and fraction notations and know the fraction and decimal equivalents for halves and fourths (e.g., $\frac{1}{2} = 0.5$ or $.50$; $\frac{7}{4} = 1\frac{3}{4} = 1.75$).

2. **Algebra and Functions 1.0** Students use and interpret variables, mathematical symbols, and properties to write and simplify expressions and sentences.

3. **Number Sense 1.5** Explain different interpretations of fractions, for example, parts of a whole, parts of a set, and division of whole numbers by whole numbers; explain equivalents of fractions (see Standard 4.0).

4. **Number Sense** **3.2** Demonstrate an understanding of, and the ability to use, standard algorithms for multiplying a multidigit number by a two-digit number and for dividing a multidigit number by a one-digit number; use relationships between them to simplify computations and to check results.

5. **Number Sense** **3.2** Demonstrate an understanding of, and the ability to use, standard algorithms for multiplying a multidigit number by a two-digit number and for dividing a multidigit number by a one-digit number; use relationships between them to simplify computations and to check results.

6. **Mathematical Reasoning 1.2** Determine when and how to break a problem into simpler parts.

Math Boxes 7◆13

1. **Measurement and Geometry 1.4** Understand and use formulas to solve problems involving perimeters and areas of rectangles and squares. Use those formulas to find the areas of more complex figures by dividing the figures into basic shapes.

2. **Measurement and Geometry 1.1** Measure the area of rectangular shapes by using appropriate units, such as square centimeter, (cm²), square meter (m²), square kilometer (km²), square inch (in²), square yard (yd²), or square mile (mi²).

3. **Algebra and Functions 1.4** Use and interpret formulas (e.g., area = length × width or $A = lw$) to answer questions about quantities and their relationships.

4. **Mathematical Reasoning 2.1** Use estimation to verify the reasonableness of calculated results.

5. **Algebra and Functions** **1.5** Understand that an equation such as $y = 3x + 5$ is a prescription for determining a second number when a first number is given.

6. **Mathematical Reasoning 1.2** Determine when and how to break a problem into simpler parts.

Math Boxes 8◆1

1. **Statistics, Data Analysis, and Probability 1.2** Identify the mode(s) for sets of categorical data and the mode(s), median, and any apparent outliers for numerical data sets.

2. **Algebra and Functions 1.0** Students use and interpret variables, mathematical symbols, and properties to write and simplify expressions and sentences.

3. **Measurement and Geometry 3.0** Students demonstrate an understanding of plane and solid geometric objects and use this knowledge to show relationships and solve problems.

4. **Statistics, Data Analysis, and Probability 2.2** Express outcomes of experimental probability situations verbally and numerically (e.g., 3 out of 4; $\frac{3}{4}$).

5. **Algebra and Functions** **2.1** Know and understand that equals added to equals are equal.

6. **Algebra and Functions** **2.2** Know and understand that equals multiplied by equals are equal.

Math Boxes 8◆2

1. **Measurement and Geometry 1.0** Students understand perimeter and area.

2. **Statistics, Data Analysis, and Probability 2.2** Express outcomes of experimental probability situations verbally and numerically (e.g., 3 out of 4; $\frac{3}{4}$).

Math Boxes 8•2 *cont.*

3. Number Sense 1.6 Write tenths and hundredths in decimal and fraction notations and know the fraction and decimal equivalents for halves and fourths (e.g., $\frac{1}{2} = 0.5$ or $.50$; $\frac{7}{4} = 1\frac{3}{4} = 1.75$).

4. Mathematical Reasoning 2.1 Use estimation to verify the reasonableness of calculated results.

5. Algebra and Functions 1.0 Students use and interpret variables, mathematical symbols, and properties to write and simplify expressions and sentences.

6. Number Sense 1.7 Write the fraction represented by a drawing of parts of a figure; represent a given fraction by using drawings; and relate a fraction to a simple decimal on a number line.

Math Boxes 8•3

1. Statistics, Data Analysis, and Probability 1.2 Identify the mode(s) for sets of categorical data and the mode(s), median, and any apparent outliers for numerical data sets.

2. Algebra and Functions 1.0 Students use and interpret variables, mathematical symbols, and properties to write and simplify expressions and sentences.

3. Measurement and Geometry 3.0 Students demonstrate an understanding of plane and solid geometric objects and use this knowledge to show relationships and solve problems.

4. Statistics, Data Analysis, and Probability 2.2 Express outcomes of experimental probability situations verbally and numerically (e.g., 3 out of 4; $\frac{3}{4}$).

5. Algebra and Functions 2.1 Know and understand that equals added to equals are equal.

6. Algebra and Functions 2.2 Know and understand that equals multiplied by equals are equal.

Math Boxes 8•4

1. Measurement and Geometry 1.0 Students understand perimeter and area.

2. Statistics, Data Analysis, and Probability 2.2 Express outcomes of experimental probability situations verbally and numerically (e.g., 3 out of 4; $\frac{3}{4}$).

3. Number Sense 1.6 Write tenths and hundredths in decimal and fraction notations and know the fraction and decimal equivalents for halves and fourths (e.g., $\frac{1}{2} = 0.5$ or $.50$; $\frac{7}{4} = 1\frac{3}{4} = 1.75$).

4. Mathematical Reasoning 2.1 Use estimation to verify the reasonableness of calculated results.

5. Algebra and Functions 1.0 Students use and interpret variables, mathematical symbols, and properties to write and simplify expressions and sentences.

6. Number Sense 1.7 Write the fraction represented by a drawing of parts of a figure; represent a given fraction by using drawings; and relate a fraction to a simple decimal on a number line.

Math Boxes 8•5

1. Number Sense 1.5 Explain different interpretations of fractions, for example, parts of a whole, parts of a set, and division of whole numbers by whole numbers; explain equivalents of fractions (see Standard 4.0).

2. Measurement and Geometry 1.4 Understand and use formulas to solve problems involving perimeters and areas of rectangles and squares. Use those formulas to find the areas of more complex figures by dividing the figures into basic shapes.

3. Number Sense 2.0 Students extend their use and understanding of whole numbers to the addition and subtraction of simple decimals.

4. Statistics, Data Analysis, and Probability 2.2 Express outcomes of experimental probability situations verbally and numerically (e.g., 3 out of 4; $\frac{3}{4}$).

5. Algebra and Functions 2.0 Students know how to manipulate equations.

6. Number Sense 3.2 Demonstrate an understanding of, and the ability to use, standard algorithms for multiplying a multidigit number by a two-digit number and for dividing a multidigit number by a one-digit number; use relationships between them to simplify computations and to check results.

Math Boxes 8•6

1. Mathematical Reasoning 2.3 Use a variety of methods, such as words, numbers, symbols, charts, graphs, tables, diagrams, and models, to explain mathematical reasoning.

2. Measurement and Geometry 1.4 Understand and use formulas to solve problems involving perimeters and areas of rectangles and squares. Use those formulas to find the areas of more complex figures by dividing the figures into basic shapes.

3. Statistics, Data Analysis, and Probability 2.2 Express outcomes of experimental probability situations verbally and numerically (e.g., 3 out of 4; $\frac{3}{4}$).

4. Mathematical Reasoning 2.0 Students use strategies, skills, and concepts in finding solutions.

5. Number Sense 3.2 Demonstrate an understanding of, and the ability to use, standard algorithms for multiplying a multidigit number by a two-digit number and for dividing a multidigit number by a one-digit number; use relationships between them to simplify computations and to check results.

Math Boxes 8•7

1. Number Sense 1.5 Explain different interpretations of fractions, for example, parts of a whole, parts of a set, and division of whole numbers by whole numbers; explain equivalents of fractions (see Standard 4.0).

2. Measurement and Geometry 1.4 Understand and use formulas to solve problems involving perimeters and areas of rectangles and squares. Use those formulas to find the areas of more complex figures by dividing the figures into basic shapes.

3. Number Sense 2.0 Students extend their use and understanding of whole numbers to the addition and subtraction of simple decimals.

Math Boxes 8·7 cont.

4. **Statistics, Data Analysis, and Probability 2.2** Express outcomes of experimental probability situations verbally and numerically (e.g., 3 out of 4; $\frac{3}{4}$).

5. **Algebra and Functions 2.0** Students know how to manipulate equations.

6. **Number Sense 3.2** Demonstrate an understanding of, and the ability to use, standard algorithms for multiplying a multidigit number by a two-digit number and for dividing a multidigit number by a one-digit number; use relationships between them to simplify computations and to check results.

Math Boxes 8·8

1. **Mathematical Reasoning 2.3** Use a variety of methods, such as words, numbers, symbols, charts, graphs, tables, diagrams, and models, to explain mathematical reasoning.

2. **Measurement and Geometry 1.4** Understand and use formulas to solve problems involving perimeters and areas of rectangles and squares. Use those formulas to find the areas of more complex figures by dividing the figures into basic shapes.

3. **Statistics, Data Analysis, and Probability 2.2** Express outcomes of experimental probability situations verbally and numerically (e.g., 3 out of 4; $\frac{3}{4}$).

4. **Mathematical Reasoning 2.0** Students use strategies, skills, and concepts in finding solutions.

5. **Number Sense 3.2** Demonstrate an understanding of, and the ability to use, standard algorithms for multiplying a multidigit number by a two-digit number and for dividing a multidigit number by a one-digit number; use relationships between them to simplify computations and to check results.

Math Boxes 8·9

1. **Algebra and Functions 2.2** Know and understand that equals multiplied by equals are equal.

2. **Number Sense 1.7** Write the fraction represented by a drawing of parts of a figure; represent a given fraction by using drawings; and relate a fraction to a simple decimal on a number line.

3. **Number Sense 3.2** Demonstrate an understanding of, and the ability to use, standard algorithms for multiplying a multidigit number by a two-digit number and for dividing a multidigit number by a one-digit number; use relationships between them to simplify computations and to check results.

4. **Number Sense 3.2** Demonstrate an understanding of, and the ability to use, standard algorithms for multiplying a multidigit number by a two-digit number and for dividing a multidigit number by a one-digit number; use relationships between them to simplify computations and to check results.

Math Boxes 9·1

1. **Mathematical Reasoning 3.0** Students move beyond a particular problem by generalizing to other situations.

2. **Algebra and Functions 1.4** Use and interpret formulas (e.g., area = length × width or $A = lw$) to answer questions about quantities and their relationships.

3. **Number Sense 3.2** Demonstrate an understanding of, and the ability to use, standard algorithms for multiplying a multidigit number by a two-digit number and for dividing a multidigit number by a one-digit number; use relationships between them to simplify computations and to check results.

4. **Mathematical Reasoning 2.4** Express the solution clearly and logically by using the appropriate mathematical notation and terms and clear language; support solutions with evidence in both verbal and symbolic work.

5. **Measurement and Geometry 3.5** Know the definitions of a right angle, an acute angle, and an obtuse angle. Understand that 90°, 180°, 270°, and 360° are associated, respectively, with $\frac{1}{4}$, $\frac{1}{2}$, $\frac{3}{4}$, and full turns.

6. **Measurement and Geometry 3.4** Identify figures that have bilateral and rotational symmetry.

Math Boxes 9·2

1. **Number Sense 1.6** Write tenths and hundredths in decimal and fraction notations and know the fraction and decimal equivalents for halves and fourths (e.g., $\frac{1}{2}$ = 0.5 or .50; $\frac{7}{4}$ = $1\frac{3}{4}$ = 1.75).

2. **Number Sense 2.1** Estimate and compute the sum or difference of whole numbers and positive decimals to two places.

3. **Algebra and Functions 1.5** Understand that an equation such as $y = 3x + 5$ is a prescription for determining a second number when a first number is given.

4. **Mathematical Reasoning 3.3** Develop generalizations of the results obtained and apply them in other circumstances.

5. **Measurement and Geometry 1.4** Understand and use formulas to solve problems involving perimeters and areas of rectangles and squares. Use those formulas to find the areas of more complex figures by dividing the figures into basic shapes.

6. **Number Sense 1.8** Use concepts of negative numbers (e.g., on a number line, in counting, in temperature, in "owing").

Math Boxes 9·3

1. **Mathematical Reasoning 3.0** Students move beyond a particular problem by generalizing to other situations.

2. **Algebra and Functions 1.4** Use and interpret formulas (e.g., area = length × width or $A = lw$) to answer questions about quantities and their relationships.

3. **Number Sense 3.2** Demonstrate an understanding of, and the ability to use, standard algorithms for multiplying a multidigit number by a two-digit number and for dividing a multidigit number by a one-digit number; use relationships between them to simplify computations and to check results.

4. **Mathematical Reasoning 2.4** Express the solution clearly and logically by using the appropriate mathematical notation and terms and clear language; support solutions with evidence in both verbal and symbolic work.

5. **Measurement and Geometry 3.5** Know the definitions of a right angle, an acute angle, and an obtuse angle. Understand that 90°, 180°, 270°, and 360° are associated, respectively, with $\frac{1}{4}$, $\frac{1}{2}$, $\frac{3}{4}$, and full turns.

Math Boxes 9•3 cont.

6. **Measurement and Geometry 3.4** Identify figures that have bilateral and rotational symmetry.

Math Boxes 9•4

1. **Number Sense 1.6** Write tenths and hundredths in decimal and fraction notations and know the fraction and decimal equivalents for halves and fourths (e.g., $\frac{1}{2} = 0.5$ or .50; $\frac{7}{4} = 1\frac{3}{4} = 1.75$).

2. **Number Sense 2.1** Estimate and compute the sum or difference of whole numbers and positive decimals to two places.

3. **Algebra and Functions (1.5)** Understand that an equation such as $y = 3x + 5$ is a prescription for determining a second number when a first number is given.

4. **Mathematical Reasoning 3.3** Develop generalizations of the results obtained and apply them in other circumstances.

5. **Measurement and Geometry 1.4** Understand and use formulas to solve problems involving perimeters and areas of rectangles and squares. Use those formulas to find the areas of more complex figures by dividing the figures into basic shapes.

6. **Number Sense (1.8)** Use concepts of negative numbers (e.g., on a number line, in counting, in temperature, in "owing").

Math Boxes 9•5

1. **Algebra and Functions (2.2)** Know and understand that equals multiplied by equals are equal.

2. **Algebra and Functions (1.3)** Use parentheses to indicate which operation to perform first when writing expressions containing more than two terms and different operations.

3. **Number Sense 1.6** Write tenths and hundredths in decimal and fraction notations and know the fraction and decimal equivalents for halves and fourths (e.g., $\frac{1}{2} = 0.5$ or .50; $\frac{7}{4} = 1\frac{3}{4} = 1.75$).

4. **Number Sense (3.2)** Demonstrate an understanding of, and the ability to use, standard algorithms for multiplying a multidigit number by a two-digit number and for dividing a multidigit number by a one-digit number; use relationships between them to simplify computations and to check results.

5. **Measurement and Geometry 1.4** Understand and use formulas to solve problems involving perimeters and areas of rectangles and squares. Use those formulas to find the areas of more complex figures by dividing the figures into basic shapes.

6. **Measurement and Geometry 3.4** Identify figures that have bilateral and rotational symmetry.

Math Boxes 9•6

1. **Statistics, Data Analysis, and Probability 2.0** Students make predictions for simple probability situations.

2. **Number Sense (1.9)** Identify on a number line the relative position of positive fractions, positive mixed numbers, and positive decimals to two decimal places.

3. **Mathematical Reasoning 2.3** Use a variety of methods, such as words, numbers, symbols, charts, graphs, tables, diagrams, and models, to explain mathematical reasoning.

4. **Algebra and Functions 1.4** Use and interpret formulas (e.g., area = length × width or $A = lw$) to answer questions about quantities and their relationships.

5. **Measurement and Geometry 1.4** Understand and use formulas to solve problems involving perimeters and areas of rectangles and squares. Use those formulas to find the areas of more complex figures by dividing the figures into basic shapes.

6. **Number Sense (1.8)** Use concepts of negative numbers (e.g., on a number line, in counting, in temperature, in "owing").

Math Boxes 9•7

1. **Algebra and Functions (2.2)** Know and understand that equals multiplied by equals are equal.

2. **Algebra and Functions (1.3)** Use parentheses to indicate which operation to perform first when writing expressions containing more than two terms and different operations.

3. **Number Sense 1.6** Write tenths and hundredths in decimal and fraction notations and know the fraction and decimal equivalents for halves and fourths (e.g., $\frac{1}{2} = 0.5$ or .50; $\frac{7}{4} = 1\frac{3}{4} = 1.75$).

4. **Number Sense (3.2)** Demonstrate an understanding of, and the ability to use, standard algorithms for multiplying a multidigit number by a two-digit number and for dividing a multidigit number by a one-digit number; use relationships between them to simplify computations and to check results.

5. **Measurement and Geometry 1.4** Understand and use formulas to solve problems involving perimeters and areas of rectangles and squares. Use those formulas to find the areas of more complex figures by dividing the figures into basic shapes.

6. **Measurement and Geometry 3.4** Identify figures that have bilateral and rotational symmetry.

Math Boxes 9•8

1. **Statistics, Data Analysis, and Probability 2.0** Students make predictions for simple probability situations.

2. **Number Sense (1.9)** Identify on a number line the relative position of positive fractions, positive mixed numbers, and positive decimals to two decimal places.

3. **Mathematical Reasoning 2.3** Use a variety of methods, such as words, numbers, symbols, charts, graphs, tables, diagrams, and models, to explain mathematical reasoning.

4. **Algebra and Functions 1.4** Use and interpret formulas (e.g., area = length × width or $A = lw$) to answer questions about quantities and their relationships.

5. **Measurement and Geometry 1.4** Understand and use formulas to solve problems involving perimeters and areas of rectangles and squares. Use those formulas to find the areas of more complex figures by dividing the figures into basic shapes.

6. **Number Sense (1.8)** Use concepts of negative numbers (e.g., on a number line, in counting, in temperature, in "owing").

Math Boxes 9◆9

1. **Algebra and Functions 2.2** Know and understand that equals multiplied by equals are equal.

2. **Algebra and Functions 1.3** Use parentheses to indicate which operation to perform first when writing expressions containing more than two terms and different operations.

3. **Number Sense 1.6** Write tenths and hundredths in decimal and fraction notations and know the fraction and decimal equivalents for halves and fourths (e.g., $\frac{1}{2} = 0.5$ or $.50$; $\frac{7}{4} = 1\frac{3}{4} = 1.75$).

4. **Number Sense 3.2** Demonstrate an understanding of, and the ability to use, standard algorithms for multiplying a multidigit number by a two-digit number and for dividing a multidigit number by a one-digit number; use relationships between them to simplify computations and to check results.

5. **Measurement and Geometry 1.4** Understand and use formulas to solve problems involving perimeters and areas of rectangles and squares. Use those formulas to find the areas of more complex figures by dividing the figures into basic shapes.

6. **Measurement and Geometry 3.4** Identify figures that have bilateral and rotational symmetry.

Math Boxes 9◆10

1. **Measurement and Geometry 3.4** Identify figures that have bilateral and rotational symmetry.

2. **Number Sense 1.8** Use concepts of negative numbers (e.g., on a number line, in counting, in temperature, in "owing").

3. **Measurement and Geometry 3.4** Identify figures that have bilateral and rotational symmetry.

4. **Mathematical Reasoning 2.2** Apply strategies and results from simpler problems to more complex problems.

5. **Number Sense 1.8** Use concepts of negative numbers (e.g., on a number line, in counting, in temperature, in "owing").

6. **Number Sense 1.8** Use concepts of negative numbers (e.g., on a number line, in counting, in temperature, in "owing").

Math Boxes 10◆1

1. **Measurement and Geometry 3.3** Identify congruent figures.

2. **Statistics, Data Analysis, and Probability 1.2** Identify the mode(s) for sets of categorical data and the mode(s), median, and any apparent outliers for numerical data sets.

3. **Number Sense 1.9** Identify on a number line the relative position of positive fractions, positive mixed numbers, and positive decimals to two decimal places.

4. **Mathematical Reasoning 2.2** Apply strategies and results from simpler problems to more complex problems.

5. **Algebra and Functions 2.0** Students know how to manipulate equations.

6. **Measurement and Geometry 1.4** Understand and use formulas to solve problems involving perimeters and areas of rectangles and squares. Use those formulas to find the areas of more complex figures by dividing the figures into basic shapes.

Math Boxes 10◆2

1. **Number Sense 1.6** Write tenths and hundredths in decimal and fraction notations and know the fraction and decimal equivalents for halves and fourths (e.g., $\frac{1}{2} = 0.5$ or $.50$; $\frac{7}{4} = 1\frac{3}{4} = 1.75$).

2. **Mathematical Reasoning 2.2** Apply strategies and results from simpler problems to more complex problems.

3. **Statistics, Data Analysis, and Probability 1.1** Formulate survey questions; systematically collect and represent data on a number line; and coordinate graphs, tables, and charts.

4. **Measurement and Geometry 2.0** Students use two-dimensional coordinate grids to represent points and graph lines and simple figures.

5. **Number Sense 1.8** Use concepts of negative numbers (e.g., on a number line, in counting, in temperature, in "owing").

Math Boxes 10◆3

1. **Statistics, Data Analysis, and Probability 1.0** Students organize, represent, and interpret numerical and categorical data and clearly communicate their findings.

2. **Algebra and Functions 1.4** Use and interpret formulas (e.g., area = length $\times$ width or $A = lw$) to answer questions about quantities and their relationships.

3. **Algebra and Functions 2.1** Know and understand that equals added to equals are equal.

4. **Measurement and Geometry 3.5** Know the definitions of a right angle, an acute angle, and an obtuse angle. Understand that 90°, 180°, 270°, and 360° are associated, respectively, with $\frac{1}{4}$, $\frac{1}{2}$, $\frac{3}{4}$, and full turns.

5. **Mathematical Reasoning 2.1** Use estimation to verify the reasonableness of calculated results.

Math Boxes 10◆4

1. **Measurement and Geometry 3.3** Identify congruent figures.

2. **Statistics, Data Analysis, and Probability 1.2** Identify the mode(s) for sets of categorical data and the mode(s), median, and any apparent outliers for numerical data sets.

3. **Number Sense 1.9** Identify on a number line the relative position of positive fractions, positive mixed numbers, and positive decimals to two decimal places.

4. **Mathematical Reasoning 2.2** Apply strategies and results from simpler problems to more complex problems.

5. **Algebra and Functions 2.0** Students know how to manipulate equations.

6. **Measurement and Geometry 1.4** Understand and use formulas to solve problems involving perimeters and areas of rectangles and squares. Use those formulas to find the areas of more complex figures by dividing the figures into basic shapes.

Math Boxes 10•5

1. **Number Sense 1.6** Write tenths and hundredths in decimal and fraction notations and know the fraction and decimal equivalents for halves and fourths (e.g., $\frac{1}{2} = 0.5$ or $.50$; $\frac{7}{4} = 1\frac{3}{4} = 1.75$).

2. **Mathematical Reasoning 2.2** Apply strategies and results from simpler problems to more complex problems.

3. **Statistics, Data Analysis, and Probability 1.1** Formulate survey questions; systematically collect and represent data on a number line; and coordinate graphs, tables, and charts.

4. **Measurement and Geometry 2.0** Students use two-dimensional coordinate grids to represent points and graph lines and simple figures.

5. **Number Sense 1.8** Use concepts of negative numbers (e.g., on a number line, in counting, in temperature, in "owing").

Math Boxes 10•6

1. **Statistics, Data Analysis, and Probability 1.0** Students organize, represent, and interpret numerical and categorical data and clearly communicate their findings.

2. **Algebra and Functions 1.4** Use and interpret formulas (e.g., area = length × width or $A = lw$) to answer questions about quantities and their relationships.

3. **Algebra and Functions 2.1** Know and understand that equals added to equals are equal.

4. **Measurement and Geometry 3.5** Know the definitions of a right angle, an acute angle, and an obtuse angle. Understand that 90°, 180°, 270°, and 360° are associated, respectively, with $\frac{1}{4}$, $\frac{1}{2}$, $\frac{3}{4}$, and full turns.

5. **Mathematical Reasoning 2.1** Use estimation to verify the reasonableness of calculated results.

Math Boxes 10•7

1. **Measurement and Geometry 1.4** Understand and use formulas to solve problems involving perimeters and areas of rectangles and squares. Use those formulas to find the areas of more complex figures by dividing the figures into basic shapes.

2. **Number Sense 1.8** Use concepts of negative numbers (e.g., on a number line, in counting, in temperature, in "owing").

3. **Mathematical Reasoning 2.1** Use estimation to verify the reasonableness of calculated results.

4. **Measurement and Geometry 1.2** Recognize that rectangles that have the same area can have different perimeters.

Math Boxes 11•1

1. **Measurement and Geometry 3.3** Identify congruent figures.

2. **Algebra and Functions 2.1** Know and understand that equals added to equals are equal.

3. **Number Sense 4.0** Students know how to factor small whole numbers.

4. **Algebra and Functions 1.3** Use parentheses to indicate which operation to perform first when writing expressions containing more than two terms and different operations.

5. **Number Sense 3.3** Solve problems involving multiplication of multidigit numbers by two-digit numbers.

Math Boxes 11•2

1. **Measurement and Geometry 3.6** Visualize, describe, and make models of geometric solids (e.g., prisms, pyramids) in terms of the number and shape of faces, edges, and vertices; interpret two-dimensional representations of three-dimensional objects; and draw patterns (of faces) for a solid that, when cut and folded, will make a model of the solid.

2. **Measurement and Geometry 3.4** Identify figures that have bilateral and rotational symmetry.

3. **Mathematical Reasoning 2.1** Use estimation to verify the reasonableness of calculated results.

4. **Algebra and Functions 1.0** Students use and interpret variables, mathematical symbols, and properties to write and simplify expressions and sentences.

5. **Number Sense 2.2** Round two-place decimals to one decimal or to the nearest whole number and judge the reasonableness of the rounded answer.

6. **Number Sense 3.3** Solve problems involving multiplication of multidigit numbers by two-digit numbers.

Math Boxes 11•3

1. **Measurement and Geometry 3.3** Identify congruent figures.

2. **Algebra and Functions 2.1** Know and understand that equals added to equals are equal.

3. **Number Sense 4.0** Students know how to factor small whole numbers.

4. **Algebra and Functions 1.3** Use parentheses to indicate which operation to perform first when writing expressions containing more than two terms and different operations.

5. **Number Sense 3.3** Solve problems involving multiplication of multidigit numbers by two-digit numbers.

Math Boxes 11•4

1. **Measurement and Geometry 3.6** Visualize, describe, and make models of geometric solids (e.g., prisms, pyramids) in terms of the number and shape of faces, edges, and vertices; interpret two-dimensional representations of three-dimensional objects; and draw patterns (of faces) for a solid that, when cut and folded, will make a model of the solid.

2. **Measurement and Geometry 3.4** Identify figures that have bilateral and rotational symmetry.

3. **Mathematical Reasoning 2.1** Use estimation to verify the reasonableness of calculated results.

4. **Algebra and Functions 1.0** Students use and interpret variables, mathematical symbols, and properties to write and simplify expressions and sentences.

5. **Number Sense 2.2** Round two-place decimals to one decimal or to the nearest whole number and judge the reasonableness of the rounded answer.

CA30

Math Boxes 11♦4 cont.

6. **Number Sense** **3.4** Solve problems involving division of multidigit numbers by one-digit numbers.

Math Boxes 11♦5

1. **Mathematical Reasoning 2.2** Apply strategies and results from simpler problems to more complex problems.

2. **Algebra and Functions 1.4** Use and interpret formulas (e.g., area = length × width or $A = lw$) to answer questions about quantities and their relationships.

3. **Statistics, Data Analysis, and Probability 2.2** Express outcomes of experimental probability situations verbally and numerically (e.g., 3 out of 4; $\frac{3}{4}$).

4. **Algebra and Functions** **1.5** Understand that an equation such as $y = 3x + 5$ is a prescription for determining a second number when a first number is given.

5. **Algebra and Functions** **1.2** Interpret and evaluate mathematical expressions that now use parentheses.

6. **Algebra and Functions 1.4** Use and interpret formulas (e.g., area = length × width or $A = lw$) to answer questions about quantities and their relationships.

Math Boxes 11♦6

1. **Measurement and Geometry 3.6** Visualize, describe, and make models of geometric solids (e.g., prisms, pyramids) in terms of the number and shape of faces, edges, and vertices; interpret two-dimensional representations of three-dimensional objects; and draw patterns (of faces) for a solid that, when cut and folded, will make a model of the solid.

2. **Measurement and Geometry 3.4** Identify figures that have bilateral and rotational symmetry.

3. **Mathematical Reasoning 2.1** Use estimation to verify the reasonableness of calculated results.

4. **Algebra and Functions 1.0** Students use and interpret variables, mathematical symbols, and properties to write and simplify expressions and sentences.

5. **Number Sense 2.2** Round two-place decimals to one decimal or to the nearest whole number and judge the reasonableness of the rounded answer.

6. **Number Sense** **3.3** Solve problems involving multiplication of multidigit numbers by two-digit numbers.

Math Boxes 11♦7

1. **Mathematical Reasoning 2.2** Apply strategies and results from simpler problems to more complex problems.

2. **Algebra and Functions 1.4** Use and interpret formulas (e.g., area = length × width or $A = lw$) to answer questions about quantities and their relationships.

3. **Statistics, Data Analysis, and Probability 2.2** Express outcomes of experimental probability situations verbally and numerically (e.g., 3 out of 4; $\frac{3}{4}$).

4. **Algebra and Functions** **1.5** Understand that an equation such as $y = 3x + 5$ is a prescription for determining a second number when a first number is given.

5. **Algebra and Functions** **1.2** Interpret and evaluate mathematical expressions that now use parentheses.

6. **Algebra and Functions 1.4** Use and interpret formulas (e.g., area = length × width or $A = lw$) to answer questions about quantities and their relationships.

Math Boxes 11♦8

1. **Number Sense** **3.3** Solve problems involving multiplication of multidigit numbers by two-digit numbers.

2. **Number Sense** **3.3** Solve problems involving multiplication of multidigit numbers by two-digit numbers.

3. **Number Sense** **3.3** Solve problems involving multiplication of multidigit numbers by two-digit numbers.

4. **Mathematical Reasoning 2.2** Apply strategies and results from simpler problems to more complex problems.

5. **Number Sense** **3.4** Solve problems involving division of multidigit numbers by one-digit numbers.

6. **Number Sense 2.2** Round two-place decimals to one decimal or to the nearest whole number and judge the reasonableness of the rounded answer.

Math Boxes 12♦1

1. **Measurement and Geometry 3.6** Visualize, describe, and make models of geometric solids (e.g., prisms, pyramids) in terms of the number and shape of faces, edges, and vertices; interpret two-dimensional representations of three-dimensional objects; and draw patterns (of faces) for a solid that, when cut and folded, will make a model of the solid.

2. **Algebra and Functions 1.4** Use and interpret formulas (e.g., area = length × width or $A = lw$) to answer questions about quantities and their relationships.

3. **Measurement and Geometry 1.0** Students understand perimeter and area.

4. **Algebra and Functions 1.0** Students use and interpret variables, mathematical symbols, and properties to write and simplify expressions and sentences.

5. **Number Sense 4.0** Students know how to factor small whole numbers.

6. **Number Sense 2.2** Round two-place decimals to one decimal or to the nearest whole number and judge the reasonableness of the rounded answer.

Math Boxes 12♦2

1. **Mathematical Reasoning 3.2** Note the method of deriving the solution and demonstrate a conceptual understanding of the derivation by solving similar problems.

2. **Mathematical Reasoning 1.1** Analyze problems by identifying relationships, distinguishing relevant from irrelevant information, sequencing and prioritizing information, and observing patterns.

3. **Algebra and Functions** **1.2** Interpret and evaluate mathematical expressions that now use parentheses.

Math Boxes 12◆2 *cont.*

4. Algebra and Functions 2.0 Students know how to manipulate equations.

5. Statistics, Data Analysis, and Probability 2.0 Students make predictions for simple probability situations.

6. Algebra and Functions 2.2 Know and understand that equals multiplied by equals are equal.

Math Boxes 12◆3

1. Measurement and Geometry 3.6 Visualize, describe, and make models of geometric solids (e.g., prisms, pyramids) in terms of the number and shape of faces, edges, and vertices; interpret two-dimensional representations of three-dimensional objects; and draw patterns (of faces) for a solid that, when cut and folded, will make a model of the solid.

2. Algebra and Functions 1.4 Use and interpret formulas (e.g., area = length × width or $A = lw$) to answer questions about quantities and their relationships.

3. Measurement and Geometry 1.0 Students understand perimeter and area.

4. Algebra and Functions 1.0 Students use and interpret variables, mathematical symbols, and properties to write and simplify expressions and sentences.

5. Number Sense 4.0 Students know how to factor small whole numbers.

6. Number Sense 2.2 Round two-place decimals to one decimal or to the nearest whole number and judge the reasonableness of the rounded answer.

Math Boxes 12◆4

1. Mathematical Reasoning 3.2 Note the method of deriving the solution and demonstrate a conceptual understanding of the derivation by solving similar problems.

2. Mathematical Reasoning 1.1 Analyze problems by identifying relationships, distinguishing relevant from irrelevant information, sequencing and prioritizing information, and observing patterns.

3. Algebra and Functions 1.2 Interpret and evaluate mathematical expressions that now use parentheses.

4. Algebra and Functions 2.0 Students know how to manipulate equations.

5. Statistics, Data Analysis, and Probability 2.0 Students make predictions for simple probability situations.

6. Algebra and Functions 2.2 Know and understand that equals multiplied by equals are equal.

Math Boxes 12◆5

1. Number Sense 3.2 Demonstrate an understanding of, and the ability to use, standard algorithms for multiplying a multidigit number by a two-digit number and for dividing a multidigit number by a one-digit number; use relationships between them to simplify computations and to check results.

2. Mathematical Reasoning 3.3 Develop generalizations of the results obtained and apply them in other circumstances.

3. Mathematical Reasoning 3.1 Evaluate the reasonableness of the solution in the context of the original situation.

4. Algebra and Functions 1.2 Interpret and evaluate mathematical expressions that now use parentheses.

5. Algebra and Functions 1.4 Use and interpret formulas (e.g., area = length × width or $A = lw$) to answer questions about quantities and their relationships.

6. Mathematical Reasoning 3.3 Develop generalizations of the results obtained and apply them in other circumstances.

Math Boxes 12◆6

1. Mathematical Reasoning 3.2 Note the method of deriving the solution and demonstrate a conceptual understanding of the derivation by solving similar problems.

2. Mathematical Reasoning 1.1 Analyze problems by identifying relationships, distinguishing relevant from irrelevant information, sequencing and prioritizing information, and observing patterns.

3. Algebra and Functions 1.2 Interpret and evaluate mathematical expressions that now use parentheses.

4. Algebra and Functions 2.0 Students know how to manipulate equations.

5. Statistics, Data Analysis, and Probability 2.0 Students make predictions for simple probability situations.

6. Algebra and Functions 2.2 Know and understand that equals multiplied by equals are equal.

Math Boxes 12◆7

1. Number Sense 3.2 Demonstrate an understanding of, and the ability to use, standard algorithms for multiplying a multidigit number by a two-digit number and for dividing a multidigit number by a one-digit number; use relationships between them to simplify computations and to check results.

2. Mathematical Reasoning 3.3 Develop generalizations of the results obtained and apply them in other circumstances.

3. Mathematical Reasoning 3.1 Evaluate the reasonableness of the solution in the context of the original situation.

4. Algebra and Functions 1.2 Interpret and evaluate mathematical expressions that now use parentheses.

5. Algebra and Functions 1.4 Use and interpret formulas (e.g., area = length × width or $A = lw$) to answer questions about quantities and their relationships.

6. Mathematical Reasoning 3.3 Develop generalizations of the results obtained and apply them in other circumstances.

Fraction Cards 1

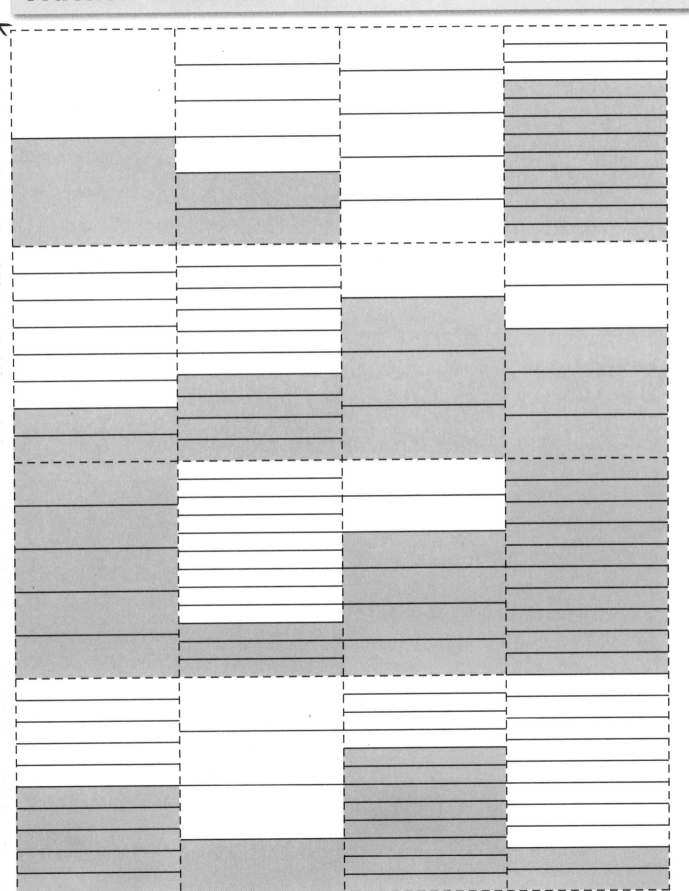

Fraction Cards 1

$$\frac{9}{} \qquad \frac{}{5} \qquad \frac{2}{} \qquad \frac{}{2}$$

$$\frac{3}{} \qquad \frac{}{4} \qquad \frac{4}{} \qquad \frac{2}{}$$

$$\frac{10}{} \qquad \frac{}{6} \qquad \frac{3}{} \qquad \frac{}{5}$$

$$\frac{2}{} \qquad \frac{}{12} \qquad \frac{1}{} \qquad \frac{}{10}$$

Activity Sheet 5

Fraction Cards 2

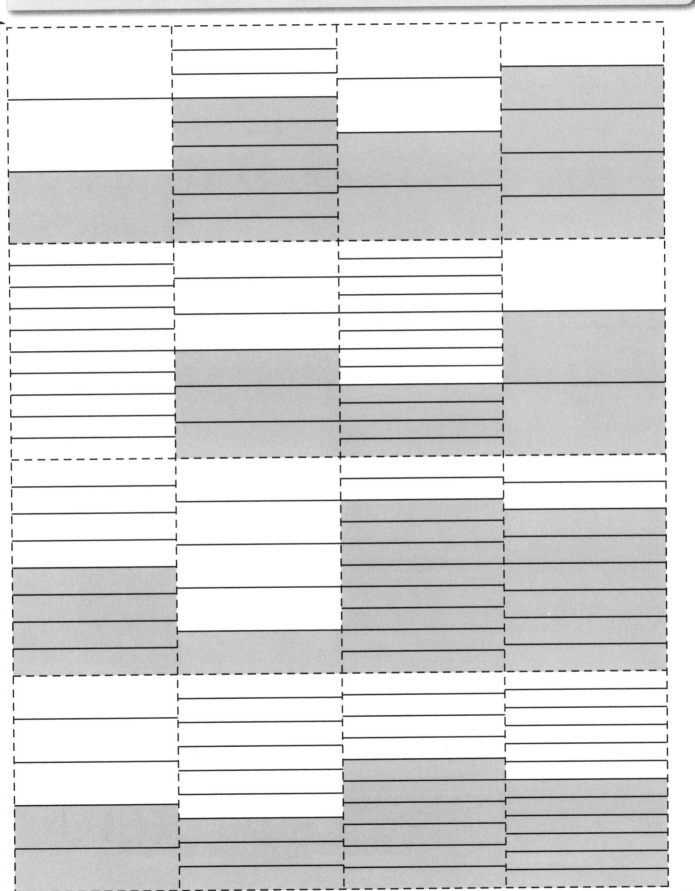

Fraction Cards 2

$$\frac{}{5} \qquad \frac{2}{} \qquad \frac{}{9} \qquad \frac{1}{}$$

$$\frac{}{3} \qquad \frac{4}{} \qquad \frac{3}{} \qquad \frac{0}{}$$

$$\frac{6}{} \qquad \frac{}{10} \qquad \frac{1}{} \qquad \frac{}{8}$$

$$\frac{}{12} \qquad \frac{6}{} \qquad \frac{}{9} \qquad \frac{2}{}$$

Activity Sheet 6

LESSON 10·2 **Dart Game**

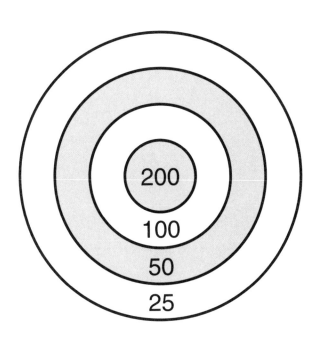

Scoreboard 1	
Player 1	Player 2

Scoreboard 2	
Player 1	Player 2

Scoreboard 3	
Player 1	Player 2

Activity Sheet 7

LESSON 10·2

Pocket-Billiards Game

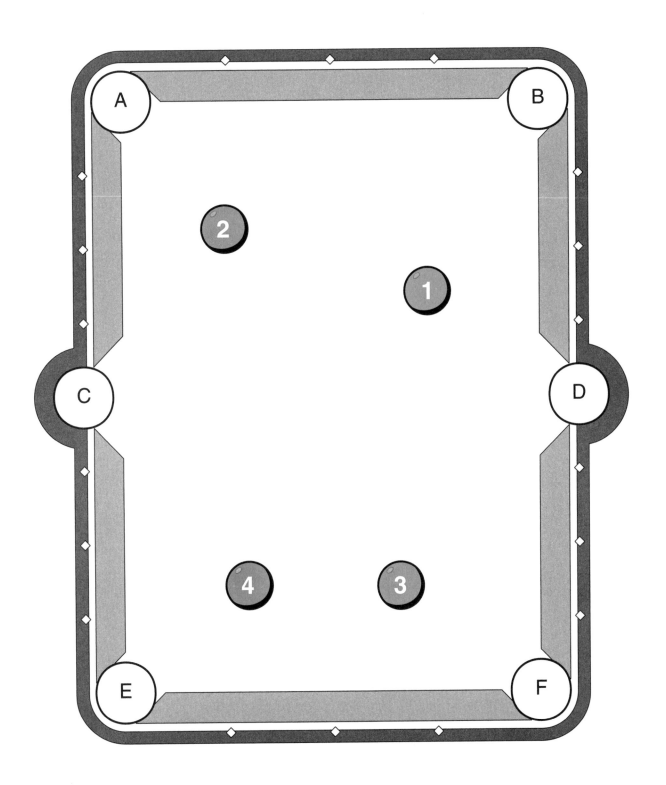